D1736618

Front cover photo – Mark Dauberman
Back cover photo – Steven Dodd Hughes

First Edition
ISBN 0-936608-84-6

Book Design – Joyce Herbst
Typesetting – John F. Michael

North Umpqua Angler's Guide

Doc Crawford

Frank Amato Publications
P.O. Box 82112 • Portland, Oregon 97282
(503) 653-8108

DEDICATION

To Dennis Solin, who had faith and put
his money where his mouth is

Photo by Bill Stormont

Doc Crawford...

...is a lifelong outdoorsman who has hiked, floated, and fished most of Oregon's rivers. He has worked as an angling guide, commercial fly tier, fishing tackle store manager, and outdoor writer. He enjoys introducing people to the sport of fishing, and has taught fly casting, fly tying, fly fishing, and steelhead fishing classes.

Doc grew up on a backwoods farm in Mississippi. He came west to Oregon in 1969, and currently lives with his wife on a small farm in Saginaw, Oregon.

CONTENTS

PREFACE

Fifteen years ago this summer, thunderstorms ran my wife and me off our planned camping itinerary in southeastern Oregon's Klamath Basin. We stuck out the first stormy night, but the second night the wind blew a limb off an old-growth fir, and the limb fell on our tent and made us wonder if we were having fun yet.

We moved over the mountain to the North Umpqua and spent the remainder of our vacation exploring new country. A bear paraded through our camp in the middle of the night and woke us up with the noise he made while using the bumper of our car for a scratching post. I hooked (and lost) a steelhead on a trout fly rod. We hiked, fished, and camped — and liked the country so well, we've spent at least a few weeks of every succeeding summer there.

The North Umpqua is world-famous, a common destination for the celebrated and the obscure, but it is also an overlooked paradise. On any summer afternoon, if there are a thousand tourists in the North Umpqua corridor, all but a few will be within a quarter of a mile of the river itself. Most will be in singledminded pursuit of a steelhead somewhere in the neighborhood of either the mouth of Steamboat Creek or Rock Creek.

There's nothing wrong with chasing a steelhead, but there is plenty wrong with chasing the crowd. Why do it when you can just as easily have a mile of river to yourself?

Which leads to what you might call a two part rule of thumb: fish like peace and quiet, and too many fishermen just like to take it easy. When you see a beaten path to the water's edge, it doesn't necessarily signify a good fishing hole; it usually just signifies a place where the water is easy to get to.

If there is a crowd of steelhead anglers whipping the river to a froth between Island Camp and Steamboat, move downriver a mile; the fishing will probably be as good or better. Better yet, give the steelhead a rest and go try your luck on Lemolo brown trout; Lemolo browns are as large (if not larger), and just as difficult to catch.

North Umpqua Angler's Guide is built around a pair of ideas: first, that the best angler is not the one who catches the most or biggest fish, but the one who has the most fun; and second, that most fishermen prefer good fishing in solitude to good fishing in the middle of a crowd.

Denise (my wife) and I travelled to the North Umpqua on the opening weekends of both the 1987 and 1988 Oregon general trout seasons. The reservoirs swarmed with bank fishermen, and the water was a traffic jam of rubber duckies, rowboats, and cabin cruisers. The easy access parts of the river were so crowded they looked the way a jelly sandwich looks after the ants find it. Denise and I fished the Clearwater River above Whitehorse Falls. The brook trout were plentiful and obliging, and we had several miles of river entirely to ourselves.

Once you've found The Place — the place where the fish are plentiful and the people are few — give yourself a break. If fishing is supposed to be fun, how come there are so many anglers willing to stand out in the hot sun, with clench-jawed glares of determination on their collective face, determined to have fun even if it kills them, making cast after unproductive cast at fish that are holed up in the shade and aren't moving for any reason? Every minute of every day will not be productive fishing time, so if the fishing is slow, do something else. Take the afternoon off. Take a nap. Go pick berries and make your tongue purple. Make one of the sidetrips described in Chapter 12. Go back to camp and play practical jokes on the camp robbers: have you ever watched how confused a squirrel can get trying to crack a rubber peanut?

Fishing the North Umpqua will be as much fun and as rewarding as you allow it to be.

Doc Crawford
Saginaw, Oregon

ACKNOWLEDGMENTS

Bill Conner, from North River Guide Service, took time off from fishing in Brookings to help me chart the river — and an angler who foregoes a fishing trip to work is rendering serious aid, indeed.

Trey Combs gave me a typewritten page of information he described as "...at least thirty years old, and I have no idea where I got it" — but it helped me considerably; and I confess to using Trey's *Steelhead Fly Fishing and Flies* as the authority on how a few steelhead fly patterns got their names.

William Jones, of Roseburg, has spent much of his life fishing the lower end of the North Umpqua and helped me with the map of the fishing holes on the lower river.

Lynn Wegand piloted me up the river in his airplane so I could take aerial photographs.

The people of the Umpqua U.S. Forest Service went out of their way to help me. They were friendly and courteous to a fault; they provided me with maps, recreation guides, information, historical data, and (occasionally) encouragement.

Ella Mae Young, of the Douglas County Historical Museum, searched out historical sources for me. She spends so much time on the run that I only saw her a few minutes during three days' research time, but she has the ability to concentrate on more than one thing at a time, and, like a good waiter, had the knack of giving me what I wanted before I asked for it.

Steven Dodd Hughes did the photography for the color plate of trout and steelhead flies.

Chapter 1

OUTFITTING YOURSELF to FISH the NORTH UMPQUA

The following is a description of the rods, reels, lines, and odds-and-ends you'll need (except terminal tackle, which is described in other chapters) to fish the North Umpqua. Some items — like sun block — are not, strictly speaking, fishing gear, but are included because they make your fishing trip less painful. The recommended rod, reel, and line combinations are geared to the fish and fishing conditions you are likely to encounter. In most cases, that means recommending what the better fishermen on the river fish with; in other cases, it means suggesting something different.

Despite the recommendations, you should have confidence in your ability to handle fish. Given the size of the average fish of each species caught along the North Umpqua, you may feel more comfortable using an outfit lighter or heavier than those recommended.

A good average North Umpqua Chinook salmon will weigh around 12 pounds, and fish that weigh in excess of 20 pounds are not uncommon. An average coho (silver) salmon will weigh about 6 to 8 pounds, and anything over 12 pounds is considered a trophy. Summer steelhead usually average about 7 pounds, but fish twice that size are not uncommon; the larger fish are usually caught by drift fishermen in the lower river. Winter steelhead average somewhat larger than summer fish (in the neighborhood of 9 or 10 pounds) and the author has seen fish up to 26 pounds caught in the lower part of the river. Rainbow and brown trout in the larger reservoirs will average about a pound, and river trout and trout caught from smaller lakes will weigh something less than a pound; brook trout will average 6 to 8 inches long. Most river-caught native cutthroat will be about 7 or 8 inches long, but fish over 12 inches are relatively common in the mainstem of the river below Rock Creek.

FLY FISHING ROD, REEL, AND LINE
An Outfit For All Occasions

There is, of course, no single outfit that will be perfectly suited to every fishing situation you encounter on the North Umpqua — but if you are limited to one fly fishing outfit, the best compromise is a 7-weight rod, 9 feet long, fitted with a reel that holds 100 yards of 20-lb. or 30-lb. test dacron backing and a weight forward floating fly line:

• While a 9-foot rod is an awkward length when fishing smaller streams and tributaries, the extra length is necessary for easy line handling when fishing the river and lakes.

• The 100 yards of dacron backing will be needed when you hook into a steelhead. Some steelhead fishermen like reels that will hold 200 or more yards of backing; the margin of safety provided by the extra backing is a comfort, and the diameter the extra line adds to the reel makes it easier to control a fighting fish. However, adding to the diameter of the reel is the only useful purpose the extra backing serves — a wading angler will very seldom land a fish that can rob him of more than 100 yards of backing. Twelve pound test backing is heavy enough to fight a steelhead, but larger diameter — 20 lb. or 30 lb. — will take up faster on a reel.

• An 8- or 9-weight line is a better choice for steelhead fishing, and a 5- or 6-weight is a better choice for trout fishing, but a 7-weight is an adequate compromise from either extreme. A sink-tip or full-sinking line is better for some steelhead fishing situations, and a full-sinking line is the only tool that will serve in some lake-fishing situations, but a weight forward floating line will suffice most of the time.

• If you are a novice at fly fishing for steelhead, you should consider using a multiplying reel. Purists frown on multiplying reels (they believe you have to suffer to have fun), but a multiplying reel will improve your chances of landing the first few fly rod steelhead you hook into. Most anglers lose the first few steelhead they hook with a single action reel because at least once before it comes to net, a steelhead will run straight at the angler, and a novice will allow the fish to get slack in the line and throw the hook. A multiplying reel helps you pick up slack line faster when a fish runs toward you.

Top the outfit off with 8-pound test leaders for steelhead fishing, 4- or 5-pound test leaders for trout fishing, a spool of light tippet material (1- or 2-pound test) for use when circumstances demand, and a selection of flies made up from the patterns described in Chapter 4.

STEELHEAD

The best fly rod steelheader the author knows — a gentleman who only fishes a few days per week, but routinely lands 30 or more fish per summer — uses a 10'6" rod, a reel that holds 150 yards of 30-pound test backing, a weight forward No. 9 fast-sinking fly line, and (depending on conditions) a 3-foot long, 6-, 8-, or 10-pound test level leader. A 9-weight outfit on a 9-foot rod is considered standard steelhead equipment on the North Umpqua, but anglers who do most of their fishing with full-sinking lines use longer rods (9'6" to 10'6"), because the extra length provides a little extra line control.

There are not many places on the North Umpqua that absolutely require a full-sinking line. A full-sinking line is necessary when fishing the deep, turbid water at the upper end of a few holes, or when fishing a slow, deep run — but in any other situation, its disadvantages outweigh its advantages. A full- sinking line is difficult to control, hard to pick up off the water, and almost impossible to mend during a drift. After a few hours, fishing a full-sinking line becomes a bull-strength battle between the line and the fisherman; the line has the advantage, because it doesn't get tired, but the fisherman does.

A sink-tip line will do the job in almost every steelhead hole on the North Umpqua, and fishing a sink-tip gives the angler much more control over the line and fly. In shallow tailouts like the one below Apple Creek or at the bottom of the Island hole, a floating line will usually suffice.

In general, the ability to spot a steelhead in a hole and place a fly within 6 inches of his nose is more important than which line or which size or pattern of fly you fish. How heavy an outfit you fish is governed by the size of fly you want to cast and the strength of the afternoon breeze you must cast it through, not by the size of fish you plan to catch. The 1/0 and larger flies some anglers use are a necessity only if the water is high, cold, or off-color; but if you enjoy fishing such large flies, a 9-weight outfit with a 10-pound or heavier leader is necessary. If, on the other hand, you prefer to fish flies with a wingspan somewhat smaller than a C-130, a 7-weight outfit with a 6- or 8-pound leader is heavy enough.

TROUT

Because of the swift current, broken water, wind-riffled surface, and general shortage of groceries, North Umpqua trout are not particularly line or leader shy. Use the heaviest leader the situation permits; a 5- or 6-pound test leader is heavier than necessary to battle a trout, but will tilt the odds in your favor if you accidentally hook a steelhead, and will inherit fewer knots from the wind. However, when fishing the lakes for trout, light leaders (3-pound test or less) are necessary.

On any afternoon, you will find yourself casting up, down, or across a stiff breeze. An 8- to 9-foot rod for a 6- or 7-weight line with a 5-pound test tapered leader 6' to 7'6" long will be easier and more comfortable to fish than a lighter weight setup. An 8-foot rod is adequate — but many good fishing holes are too deep to wade, and the brush grows right to the water's edge. In such a situation, the 9-foot rod is preferable: it allows longer, easier, better controlled roll casts, and better line control when the line is on the water.

A floating line will suffice when fishing waters up to waist deep, or when the fish are feeding on or near the surface. In the middle of the day, when the trout have gone deeper to escape the sun, a sink-tip line will put the fly down to the trout's level in the river, and a full-sinking line may be required for lake fishing.

SPINNING/CASTING ROD, REEL, AND LINE

A fly angler has to have a balanced outfit, or it simply won't work. No such limitations apply to spinning and casting gear, and the angler can make do with outrageously mismatched rod, reel, and line combinations, and still have fun and catch fish. However, the following outfits are generally accepted as standard on the North Umpqua:

REELS

Most salmon and steelhead anglers use level-wind reels. A spinning reel is easy to use and will make an instant expert caster of an angler, but that single advantage is outweighed by the spinning reel's two disadvantages: no matter how new or improved, a spinning reel still twists the line; and a mediocre level-wind will have a more reliable drag system than even the best, most carefully engineered spinning reel.

At the end of a day's fishing, lake trollers who use spinning reels remove the terminal tackle, strip out the first 100 feet of line on the reel, and troll just the line behind the boat for a few minutes to relieve the twist the spinning reel caused.

When fishing for steelhead or salmon, most anglers will use an 8' to 8'6" rod designed for 8- to 12-pound test line, but the author prefers a 7'6" rod. The shorter rod will still throw a lure across the river when necessary — but it also allows more accurate casts and is less in the way when fishing from a boat.

The reel will be filled with 8-pound test line (sometimes fished with a 6-pound test leader) when the quarry is summer steelhead or silver salmon. Because winter fish are usually heavier than their summer cousins, and because the water isn't as clear as in summer, most anglers use 10- to 14-pound test line for winter fishing.

Some anglers feel more comfortable with 17- to 20-pound test line when Chinook salmon are in the river, but the heavier line can cause more problems than it solves. The rule of thumb is: with light line, you lose more fish, but you also hook more; with heavy line, you lose fewer fish, but you also get fewer strikes. If there are plenty of fish in the river, the size of line you use isn't critical — but if conditions are bad, and fishing is hard, the line you use can make the difference between getting a few strikes (on light line), or getting skunked (using heavy line).

Most anglers who spin fish for trout prefer ultralight gear — short, fairy wand rods fitted with ultralight reels and 2-pound test line. Ultralight gear will handle the trout in North Umpqua tributaries, but is too light for fishing the reservoirs and the main stem of the river. There are no steelhead above Soda Springs Dam, but Lemolo Lake holds brown trout as large as summer steelhead. Occasionally, an afternoon's casual trout fishing on the river is interrupted by a steelhead who grabs the lure and makes a scene because nobody bothered to inform him he wasn't invited; to be prepared for such an eventuality, load the reel with line which suits your gear to the fish you might catch, rather than the fish you expect to catch. A spinning outfit consisting of a 7-foot light action rod, fitted with a reel that holds at least 100 yards of 6-pound test line, is light enough to keep the fun in trout fishing the river or any of its lakes, but heavy enough to give you a fighting chance at landing an errant steelhead.

LICENSE, TAG, SYNOPSIS AND MAP

Oregon's synopsis of angling regulations is more than 30 pages long. Legal tackle and methods, which species you may fish for, legal size limits, and bag limits, all may vary from stream to stream and from place to place on a particular stream. So, whenever you fish in Oregon, you should have at hand a current angling license (and salmon/steelhead tag), a current *Synopsis of Oregon Sport Fishing Regulations,* and a map of the area you plan to fish. The license and tag make you legal, and, with luck and frequent consultation, the synopsis and map keep you legal.

OTHER EQUIPMENT

WADERS

Waders are merely a convenience for spin fishermen, who can stand in a thicket and cast across the river, but are very nearly a necessity for fly anglers.

River trout are plentiful enough to be caught at will without ever getting your feet wet, but if you want to catch steelhead you have to suffer. Suffer means wade an ice-cold river. As a matter of course, most anglers buy chest waders, but few understand their limitations — that is, keeping you dry in knee-deep water. In sedate streams (like Henry's Fork on the Harriman Ranch) you can safely wade water that comes within an inch of the top of chest waders; but except in a very few relatively sedate stretches, wading more than knee-deep in the North Umpqua is suicidal.

The North Umpqua is a very swift, high-gradient stream, and most of its bed is either cobble to boulder sized rocks, or bedrock — and in every case, extremely treacherous wading. The rocks are coated with algal slime, and the current in shin-deep water is usually strong enough to knock you off your feet if you slip. Under such dangerous conditions, you should wear waders with grip soles, use good wading technique, and limit your wading to shallow waters.

Some anglers prefer metal-cleat or caulk-soled waders, but the author prefers felt soles on the North Umpqua. Metal cleats last longer, but are heavier and don't offer the same degree of comforting, certain traction.

Anytime you wade in swift water, or water more than shin-deep, you should use a wading staff. Several types are for sale at fishing tackle shops, and if you don't want or can't afford those, you can make one for yourself: cut a limb or a sapling long enough that, when stood on end, will reach almost to your armpits, and strong enough that it won't break when you lean your full weight on it. Notch it a few inches from the large end, and tie on a loop of heavy cord long enough to go over your shoulder (the cord allows you to let go of the staff while fishing, without losing it).

When wading, ...shuffle, don't walk. Pretend your wading staff is a third leg. Never try to move one foot past the other, as you do when walking. Use the wading staff to probe forward, to make sure you aren't stepping off into a deep hole. Balance your weight on one foot and the staff, slide the other foot forward, transfer your balance to the staff and the forward foot, then drag the rear foot forward. At the completion of each move forward, you should be braced like the three legs of a tripod, with the wading staff as the downstream leg. If the current is coming from your left, lead off with your left foot and drag your right foot behind it; if the current is from your right, lead off with your right foot and drag your left. Try to leave yourself a downstream exit route in any hole you wade; wading at even a shallow upstream angle can be difficult in the North Umpqua.

If you are wearing chest waders, you should have a wading belt tightened around the outside of them, a few inches below the top. If you plan to wade in swift water more than knee deep, you should wear a life preserver. The North Umpqua is always cold, so if you are prone to cramping, don't wade for at least an hour after eating, and don't wade deep, swift water at all.

The author prefers to limit himself to waters that can be waded in hip waders; even so, he has averaged about one dunking per season on the North Umpqua. Limiting oneself to waters that can easily be waded in hip waders reduces the total area of fishable water by about one-third and reduces the probability of drowning in a wading accident to very nearly zero.

The new generation of skin-tight foam waders makes taking a dunking less dangerous than it once was — but you shouldn't allow the extra margin of safety lull you into taking unnecessary chances.

The stout-hearted can wade wet (that is, without waders) in tolerable comfort from the middle of June to the end of trout season.

RUBBER DUCKY

The backcountry lakes — the ones you have to hike into — offer some of the best trout fishing in the North Umpqua region. However, most of these lakes can only be fished effectively from a boat. Rubber Ducky is a nickname (coined as an insult) for small, inexpensive inflatable boats. These small inflatables are relatively safe to use on lakes, but are not safe and should not be used in the river.

More than a decade ago, Orvis advertised a small inflatable boat that cost more than $100; because of economies of scale and improvements in technology, you can now buy an inflatable of comparable quality for about $80. The author's two-man Sevylor, with oars, foot pump, and patch kit, weighs a few ounces over 14 pounds — which means a backpack can be loaded with the boat and all the other gear needed for a three-day weekend fishing trip and still weigh in at less than 35 pounds.

Many of the high-country lakes in the North Umpqua drainage are ideal for float tube fishing, but a float tube, waders, and flippers will usually weigh more and take up more space than a rubber ducky — so the extra weight and bulk rule them out as backpacking gear.

FISHING VEST

If you are trekking into an untamed wilderness, three days removed from the nearest source of supplies,

wear a fishing vest; if you are fishing the North Umpqua, leave the vest locked away in camp. As treacherous as the North Umpqua is to wade, you can expect to fall in and get soaked at least a few times every season; if you are wearing a vest with all the tackle you own zippered into its pockets, you'll spend the next few days after a dunking trying to get your gear dry.

Instead, wear lightweight shirts with button-down pockets. With a little planning you can fit everything you need for a morning or afternoon's fishing into two shirt pockets — and then, when you fall in, an hour spread out in the sun will fluff-dry everything but your aplomb.

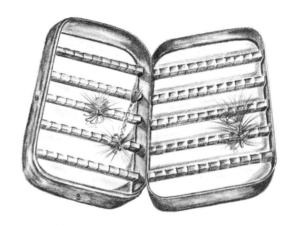

FLY BOXES

Most fly anglers prefer compartmented plastic boxes, but when fishing swift rivers like the North Umpqua, your flies are protected better by aluminum point-clip boxes (of the type made by Perrine or Wheatley). If you use aluminum point-clip boxes, the flies must be plucked one at a time from the clips (and can't accidentally fall out of the box) and the box itself can be made virtually loss-proof with a safety pin and a length of monofilament line (thread a piece of 30-pound test monofilament line through one of the ventilation holes in the box, and tie a small plastic bead to one end, and a brass safety pin to the other; when carrying the box in a pocket, hook the safety pin to the pocket's hem).

Both Perrine and Wheatley also make dry fly boxes that have a lid on each individual compartment, so to remove one, you needn't expose an entire boxful of flies and chance losing them. Other manufacturers (notably Flambeau) make foam-lined soft plastic boxes that can be used to carry wet or dry flies. If you like gaudy colors, Scientific Anglers makes a plastic clip box suitable for large wet patterns.

GADGETS

The most important gadget to be found in an angler's pocket is a hook sharpener. The cheapest imported junk fly will catch a fish if the hook is sharp, but the best tie on a best-quality forged hook will not catch a fish if the point is dull.

The author uses a small, flexible, grit-impregnated epoxy point file available in most auto parts stores and some tackle shops: the point file (unlike steel files) doesn't rust, weighs virtually nothing, costs less than a dollar, is almost unbreakable, and can be strung on a keychain with the other gadgets described below (to make it harder to lose).

Of all the other gadgets a fishermen might decorate his shirtfront with, the most useful are nail clippers or Pal angler's clip, safety pin (for punching excess head cement out of fly eyes, and picking wind knots out of leaders), and a hemostat (to use as a hook remover, and to pick small flies out of a box and hold them steady while being tied to a leader). All three can be strung on a key chain, and safely depended to your shirt pocket with the safety pin. If you use a paste fly floatant packaged in a pop-top plastic can, the floatant can also be strung on the chain.

A good pocketknife is the most universally useful of all tools; it should have a handle that fits your hand comfortably, and a sharp blade made of steel that will hold an edge. It should have a blade long enough to split an apple in half in one cut, and be comfortable enough to handle to peel and core a dozen apples, one after the other, without getting a cramp in your hand. With such a knife, you can do any cutting job from carving kindling to butchering a fish. If you plan to kill fish, a fillet knife with a narrow, thin blade about 6 inches long is a useful addition to your kit bag. The scabbarded monstrosities you see hanging from pilgrims' belts in campgrounds aren't much good for anything but dragging the wearer's pants down.

Polarized sunglasses are an absolute necessity for North Umpqua summer steelhead fishing. With polarized glasses, your eyes will remain relatively rested for an entire day's fishing, and you'll be able to spot a fish precisely in a hole, and know exactly where to cast your fly for best effect. Without polarized glasses, you'll be fishing blind all day — fishing to the water rather than to the fish — and you'll end your day on the river with bloodshot eyes and a headache.

A straw hat will help keep your temper and your head cool — and if an errant puff of wind grabs your backcast, the fly will bury itself in the hat instead of your earlobe. Put a chin string on the hat, so you won't lose it when the breeze blows it off your head.

And never go anywhere in western Oregon without raingear. Raingear seems to be the one item you never need unless you forgot it at home. On the North Umpqua, rain is a probability on Memorial Day weekend and every day between the fifteenth of October and the first of June, and a possibility any other day. If you plan to fish during the rainy season, a raincoat with elasticized cuffs will earn its keep, keeping your casting arm dry.

CAMERA

A good camera can help you preserve the memories of the fish you catch on the North Umpqua. The most versatile camera is a 35mm with as few automatic features as possible (the more automatic it is, the more gear trains there are to break down — and no quick repairs are possible in the field).

Use the fastest speed film available; the new high-speed color films are not as grainy as you might expect. Eastman Kodak's ASA 1000 will produce sharp, good quality enlargements up to about 6x8 if you start with a good negative.

If you plan to take many photographs, wear brightly colored clothes. Late in the season, when the leaves have begun to change and the whole out-of-doors assaults you with technicolor, you'll get lost in your own picture if you wear dull-colored clothing.

KNAPSACK

Much of the better fishing along the North Umpqua is best accessible by trail. Hike a mile down a trail in the heat of the summer with waders on, and you'll swelter. Roll the waders up and carry them and a thermos of cold drinks to the river in a knapsack, and you'll arrive cool and (almost) ready to fish.

FLY FLOATANT AND LEADER SINK

Only rarely will you need a fly floatant on the North Umpqua — the few dry fly situations you'll face are described in other chapters — but you should have it on hand. Any commercial floatant will do the job; the best one, if you can find such an animal, is the one that doesn't melt and leak all over you on a hot day.

Leader sink compounds are surfactants — that is, they make your leader sink by breaking up the surface tension of the water. Buy a container of leader sink if it makes you comfortable, but (if you are camping) you have an inexpensive, effective leader sink compound at hand in the form of the liquid soap used for dishwashing. Use one of the unscented brands — the perfumes in some brands attract fish, and using them could, by stretching a point, be considered bait fishing.

LANDING GEAR

If you plan to release fish, the less you handle it the better, and the only landing gear you need is a hook remover.

If you plan to kill fish, you need something to land it with. Trout can be landed by hand or with a small net. Although difficult to find, tailing gloves are a treasure, the surest and easiest way for a wading angler to land a fish. Tailing gloves were actually developed for use in fish canneries; the fingers and palm of the glove are lined with minute metal spikes that cut through the slime on a fish's skin and allow you to get a good grip on a live fish. To land a fish with a tailing glove, lead it into calm water and grasp it firmly by its caudal peduncle (the narrow part of its body, next to the tail).

If you can't find a tailing glove in your local tackle or hardware store, a G.I. surplus woolen glove liner is fully as comfortable to wear and (if you have a strong grip) will tail a fish almost as well.

When you fish from a boat, use a landing net. Use the largest net you can find for landing salmon or steelhead; many fish are lost when brought to the net because the net is too small. To land a large fish with a net, maneuver the played-out fish to a spot where the net can be held downstream of it, then ease off the pressure from the rod, and the fish drifts backward into the net of its own accord. Brought to net thusly, if the fish feels the net and makes a panic run, there is less chance of dislodging the hook and losing the fish.

Once the fish is landed, it should be killed. Allowing a fish to flop around in a creel or fish box and die slowly is immoral and inexcusable, and far fewer anglers would do it if fish knew how to scream. The cleanest way to kill a fish is to strike it sharply on the head, above its eyes. The handle of a pocketknife is heavy enough to do the job on trout, but a billy an inch or so in diameter and a foot long is required to do the job on salmon and steelhead.

PROTECTION FROM BITES AND BLISTERS

The most persistent enemy you face while fishing is the sun; expose yourself to it long enough, and you will develop skin cancer. Both direct rays and the light reflected from the water will burn you. To protect yourself, wear a hat, sunglasses, a lightweight long-sleeved shirt, and a sun-block cream on your nose. If you prefer baseball caps to hats, wear the type that has a curtain on the back (like a Foreign Legion kepi), to protect the back of your neck. Carry a moisturizing stick in your pocket for protecting chapped lips.

In 15 years' fishing on and around the North Umpqua, the author has never encountered a poisonous snake. There possibly are rattlesnakes in the region, but if you watch where you put your hands and feet, you are not likely to be bitten.

However, the North Umpqua does have its pantheon of noxious pests: black widow spiders, yellow jackets, hornets, bees, horseflies, deerflies, blackflies, mosquitoes, ticks, chiggers, no-see-ums, ants, and other bugs less susceptible of identification.

Black widows are shy creatures, partial to dark corners, crannies, and holes; keep your hands out of such places, and you are not likely to get bitten. Most other insects can be kept at bay with a combination of insect repellant and clean camping habits. When on the trail, hiking to a backcountry lake, you may find that, since perspiration washes insect repellant off, a long-sleeved shirt and G.I. surplus mosquito headnet offers more protection than liquid repellant. A handful of brush used like a swatter, the way a horse uses his tail, can also help you keep the bugs moving.

Since the North Umpqua also has its share of poison oak, you should have a bottle of calamine lotion stowed somewhere among your gear.

Scott Ripley carefully releases a wild steelhead. Irene Ripley photo

Chapter 2

TERMINAL TACKLE and TACTICS

SPINNING ROD "FLY FISHING ONLY"

From the marker near the mouth of Rock Creek upstream to Soda Springs Dam, the North Umpqua is restricted to fly fishing only. On the North Umpqua, fly fishing only developed as a conservation method — a way of reducing angling pressure and giving the anadromous fish runs a chance to recover from the snagging and "DuPont spinners" (dynamite) that once were so popular throughout the system.

You may fish the "fly fishing only" section of the river with any type of rod and reel and use a floating plastic bubble for a casting weight, provided the lure on the business end of the rig is a traditional artificial fly. (There are occasional minor changes in the regulations, so make sure you read the synopsis of angling regulations currently in effect before using this method of fishing).

DRIFT FISHING TACTICS

HOOK AND LEADER

Salmon and steelhead fishermen use an extra heavy, extra short shank hook (any of dozens of styles including an Eagle Claw Beak or Baithold hook, Seiko Comet, Mustad No. 92167, or Gamakatsu Octopus will suffice). These hooks are available with turned-up or turned-down eyes, and with or without a slice (bait-holding barb) on the shank. Most fishermen use hooks without the sliced shank for tying an egg-loop snell, because the slice can nick the line and weaken the knot. Many fishermen tie egg-loop snells on all their salmon and steelhead hooks, because the snell knot cushions the strain a leader must take, and fewer fish break off. Sizes 1 and 1/0 hooks are adequate for most fishing, but some fishermen go as large as a No. 3/0 hook snelled on a 17-pound test leader when fishing for Chinook, and as small as a No. 4 hook on a 6-pound test leader when fishing for summer steelhead.

In an average day's fishing, you will probably lose a dozen leader rigs. Tying up a few dozen egg-loop snell leaders the night before a fishing trip will save time, and on winter days when your hands are so cold your fingers don't work right, will save frustration. To keep the leaders from causing a tangle in your tackle box, they can be kept in a leader dispenser made for that purpose, and sold at most tackle stores, or can be wound on a piece of cardboard, or coiled individually and kept in small zipper-lock plastic bags. Outfit each leader with a small bright-colored plastic bead above the hook, and a short piece of fluorescent yarn (red and chartreuse are the favored colors on the North Umpqua). The yarn is simply an extra attractant, and makes the bait more visible in off-color water; the plastic bead adds a little extra attractant to the bait, and also acts as a ball bearing when you fish spinning drift lures like Birdie Drifters or Glo-Gos.

FLOATING LURES

Among the more effective artificial lures are the floating lures — Okie and Birdie Drifters, Corkies, Glo-Gos, and Spin-n-Glos. These lures can be fished by themselves, or with eggs. The lure should be rigged as illustrated, with a bead on the leader between the lure and hook; the bead serves as a ball bearing for the spinning type lures, and slightly increases the distance from the lure to the hook point, which increases your chances of a solid hook-up when you set the hook on a fish.

One style of drifter is about as effective as another in swift water; in slower water, the spinning types — Birdie, Glo-Go, and Spin-n-Glo — are more effective. In most situations, the mottled colors that more closely resemble natural eggs (pink pearl and clown) are more effective; of the solid colors, the original Okie orange is probably the best; other, brighter colors, and fluorescent colors, are reserved for times when the water is murky and the fluorescence is needed to make the lure visible.

The size of the lure is governed by the fishing conditions. When the water is low and clear, a small drifter,

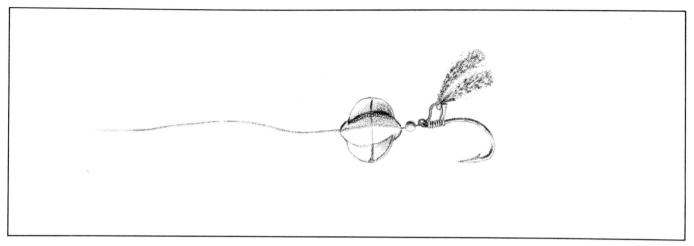

no larger than a single salmon egg, may produce the best. If you are bumping eggs, the addition of a drifter lure slightly smaller than the cluster of eggs on your hook will help float the eggs and keep them from hanging up on bottom. However, you should not, at any time, use a drifter lure larger than the gap of the hook — these lures are hard, and large ones will obstruct the hook point when you set the hook.

FISHING WITH EGGS AND SAND SHRIMP

The most commonly used bait is cluster eggs — salmon or steelhead eggs still on the skein (the word skein can refer either to roe still on the ribbon as it comes from the hen fish, or to the membrane that holds the ribbon of eggs together). Commercially cured eggs are sold by the pound or skein at most sporting goods outlets on the part of the river below the "fly fishing only" area. Once a package of eggs is opened, the contents should be protected, as much as possible, from heat, used as soon as possible, and refrigerated between fishing trips.

Sooner or later, you'll get lucky, and land a hen fish laden with eggs. If you plan to use the eggs within 2 or 3 weeks, the only cure needed to preserve them is a sprinkling of table salt. If you want to save the eggs for more than a few weeks, the following recipe will preserve them for up to 2 years:

Thoroughly mix 3 cups borax, 2 cups sugar, and 1 cup salt. Roll the skeins of eggs in the mix, and lay them out on newspaper (the newspaper soaks up the moisture leaching out of the eggs). Every few hours, roll the skeins over onto a dry spot, and sprinkle on more cure. After about 8 hours, pack the eggs in pint jars or heat-sealed plastic freezer bags. Keep refrigerated (not frozen).

Some anglers cut the cured skeins of eggs into bait-sized chunks before packing them away, but doing so is wasteful. When you cut a chunk of bait off a skein, you cut eggs in two. If you cut the skeins up before curing, the juice from the broken eggs leaches out into the cure; if you wait and cut bait off as needed on the stream, the juice from the broken eggs goes into the river and makes the eggs milk better. "Milk" is the term used for the white juice that leaks from the eggs and attracts the fish.

Many anglers habitually use too much bait when fishing with cluster eggs; the bait should be just large enough to cover the hook — a chunk perhaps the size of the end of your thumb. To get the bait onto the hook properly, thread the bait onto the hook, making sure the hook passes through the skein at least twice, push a loop of leader down through the eye of the hook (the "egg loop"), wrap the loop of line around the eggs and hook, and pull tight.

If you are an angler who has patience and a high tolerance for boredom, you may try "plunking" — that is, stick a sizable gob of eggs on the hook, tie enough weight on the rig to anchor it to the bottom, fling it out into the middle of the river, and forget about it until a fish tries to take it away from you.

Plunking is an effective method of catching salmon and steelhead. Plunk for steelhead when the water is either rising or already high, and discolored enough you can't see the bottom in waist-deep water; under those conditions, the fish will be moving steadily upstream, rather than holding up during daylight hours, as they do under lower water conditions. Cast the rigging into a deep hole at the bottom of a rapids; make the cast far enough upstream so the bait comes to rest under the point where the standing waves settle down into flat water. When fishing for Chinook, plunk the bait in the deepest part of the hole. Chinook will keg up in a hole, but may go for hours without biting, then go on the bite for only a few minutes. Experiment a little, and try to find the place where you occasionally feel a fish collid-

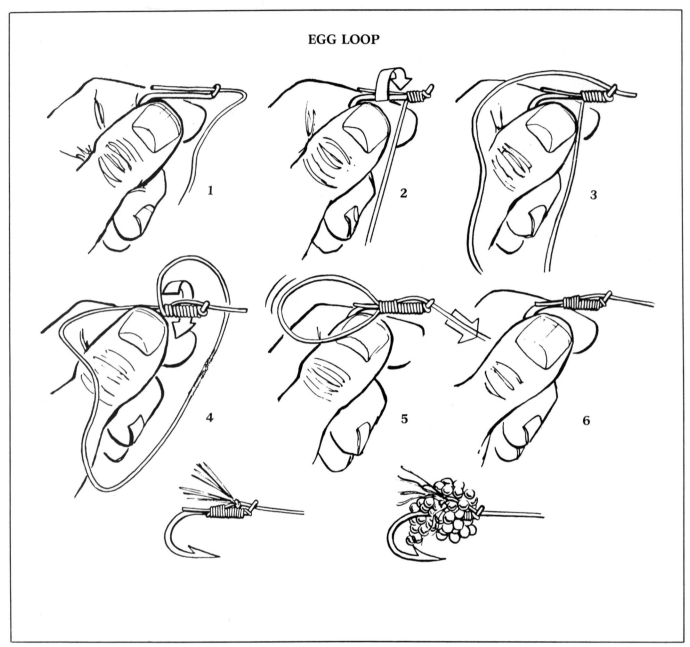

EGG LOOP

ing with your line; once you've settled your bait rig where the fish are, forget about it, and the fish will eventually pick it up.

However, most anglers would rather "drift fish" — that is, cast the bait out and let it bump along the bottom down through a hole. The keys to effective drift fishing are casting the bait to the right part of a hole, and using the right amount of weight.

Since salmon and steelhead have slightly different habits, what constitutes "the right part of the hole" depends on which one you are after. While migrating upstream, Chinook will almost invariably hold in the deepest part of the hole; if you see a Chinook in shallow water, it probably is either spawning, or has already

spawned and is waiting to die; in either case, it isn't proper prey for an angler. In long, deep holes, steelhead prefer to hold around boulders or to either side of the main current in the bottom half of the hole. In smaller holes, the steelhead will hold under the point where standing waves subside into flat water.

The right amount of weight is enough to take the bait to the bottom and keep it bumping along the bottom without hanging up; if you thread a small bobber (an Okie- or Corkie-type lure) on the leader, it will help float the hook and eggs and keep the hook from hanging up. The terminal rigs shown in the illustration have evolved over decades of fishing, and are less likely to hang up on bottom than sinkers clamped on the line. Oldtimers say,

"If you aren't losing rigging hanging up on the bottom, you're not doing it right" – but if you are losing a rig every cast, that also is not doing it right. You should be able to feel the weight bump the bottom 2 or 3 times per second; less weight won't put the bait in the fish-catching zone, and more weight will lose more tackle than is necessary. Since the current is never exactly the same in any two holes, you'll have to adjust the amount of weight you use every time you move.

Anglers who fish from a drift boat have other tactics at their command. Bumping or back-bouncing is a variation of drift fishing: instead of casting from one side, the angler anchors his boat above a drift, and "bumps" the eggs along the bottom down through the hole. Bumping requires a level-wind reel and a little more weight than usual on the rigging; the angler lowers the rigging to the bottom, and, with the reel on freespool and his thumb on the spool, lifts the tip of his rod to get the bait off the bottom, takes his thumb off the spool until the weight hits bottom again, and repeats the procedure until the bait reaches the lower end of the hole.

The three keys to successful bumping are the water you fish, how much weight you use, and how you handle the rod. You "bump" holes that are too deep for pulling plugs (more than a dozen feet deep) or too roily to drift fish. You carry several different sizes of sinkers, and adjust the amount of weight on your rigging so each time you pick it up it takes about a second to touch bottom again. Use too little weight, and the rigging won't bump solidly on bottom; use too much weight, and you'll tend to pick the tip of your rod up too high trying to make the rigging bounce. When bumping, keep your thumb on the reel spool; as you pick the rod tip up to lift the weight off the bottom, if you feel resistance, set the hook. Keep the rod tip low – Chinook, especially, have hard mouths, and you must set the hook solidly; and if the rod tip is straight up, you have no place to go to set the hook.

Deep, roily holes will have eddies on the bottom just like the ones on the surface – places where there seems to be little or no current – and salmon tend to congregate in these deep water eddies; so when you find such a spot, fish it hard.

Holes deep enough to backbump can also be fished with a diving bait rig. Attach a small diver – a Jet Planer or a Hot-n-Tot with the hooks removed – to your line; use an 18- to 24-inch leader tipped with a treble hook, thread a cluster of eggs onto the leader in such a way that the leader passes through the skein, and the cluster of eggs is cradled in the treble hook; tie the leader to the belly eye on the diver. Fish the rig through a deep hole the same way you would fish a plug in shallower water.

Rolling Shot is a way of covering long, slower-moving stretches of water – places you don't expect to hold fish, but want to drift your bait through just in case. Shot rollers pinch 3 or 4 split shot onto the line above the swivel; they can then cast out to one side of the boat and hold the boat back so the rigging rolls down the bottom of the river abreast of the boat. In stretches of the river where the current is constant and the bottom is uniform, a practiced shot roller can keep his bait moving without hanging up on the bottom for 100 yards or more.

Most wild steelhead should be returned to the river to maintain a strong spawning population. Scott Ripley photo

Live sand shrimp are an effective bait. Sand shrimp are a small crustacean dug from coastal beaches and trucked inland. Before you buy a container of sand shrimp, open the lid and make sure the shrimp are alive; sand shrimp lose their effectiveness as bait when they die.

They are a fragile bait, and tear off the hook easily. Generally, the first angler of the day using sand shrimp in a fishing hole will catch the most fish; after several anglers have fished the hole, enough shrimp have torn off hooks and are crawling around on the bottom of the hole to make any one bait get lost in the crowd. There are ways to reduce the number of baits you lose from tearing off the hook. A sand shrimp has claws and a three-lobed tail, like its freshwater cousin, the crawfish; it will stay on the hook better, and fish will take it more readily, if you carry a small pair of scissors and snip off the claws and the 2 outer lobes of the tail. A sand shrimp is

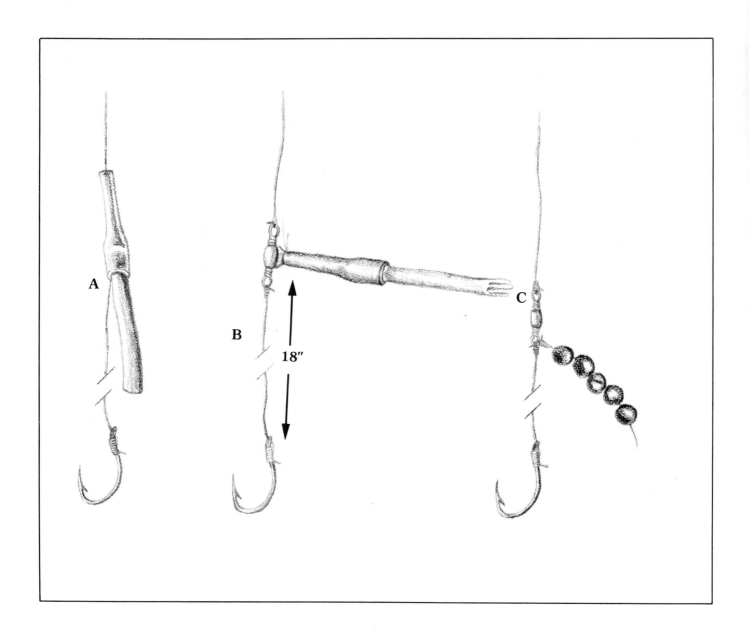

18"

usually hooked through the tail; hooking it through the thorax or head, or threading it on like an earthworm will kill it. It will live longer and stay on the hook better if, rather than impaling it, you attach it to the hook with a rubber band.

OTHER BAITS

Other salmon and steelhead baits you may occasionally see used on the North Umpqua include cocktail shrimp, crawfish tails, clam strips, and earthworms (for summer steelhead). All four will catch fish if you work at it hard enough, but none are as effective as sand shrimp and cluster eggs.

Some trout fishermen like to fish for trout and summer steelhead with single salmon eggs, and the fragility of single eggs demand a special 4X or 5X short, light-wire hook (Eagle Claw 38R or Mustad 9651). The effectiveness of single eggs can occasionally be increased by stringing a small fluorescent orange bead on the leader (5/32 or less; larger beads will interfere with the hook).

When fishing adult stoneflies or grasshoppers, some fishermen use Baithold hooks, but a light-wire Aberdeen hook (Eagle Claw No. 215A Cricket hook or its equivalent) works better. The full length of the bug can be wormed onto the light wire hook. Use a plastic bubble for casting weight, and, because of the hook's light weight, the bug will still float and can be fished the way a fly fisherman fishes a dry fly.

Grasshoppers and crickets are most easily caught

early in the morning when still sluggish from the night chill in the air.

A small (No. 14 or No. 16) single egg or baithold hook works better when fishing nymphs or grubs. Hook the the bait once through the thorax. White grubs can be collected from under the bark of downed fir or pine trees; find a tree that has been down just long enough for the bark to slip, pull the bark off in slabs, and the grubs will be found in the sawdust between the bark and the bole. Local anglers call stonefly nymphs hellgrammites; in the part of the river where stoneflies are plentiful, hellgrammites can be collected easily during the first few hours the sun is on the water by turning over rocks and deadwood in shallow riffles.

In the high lakes, cheese or other doughball-type baits are occasionally used. Use a small (size 14 or 16) treble hook, and, with your fingers, mold on a small ball of yellow cheese or bread.

When the bottom of a lake is covered with weeds, a floating bait rig improves the fishing. A floating bait rig consists of a leader at least 30 inches long, and a long-shank hook with a night crawler wormed on and a miniature marshmallow stuck on the point. The marshmallow floats the bait up out of the weeds, and adds a little color to make the bait more attractive to the fish. Marshmallows sold for bait may be dyed any of several colors, but red and chartreuse seem to be the most productive.

The average trolling tackle encountered on Toketee or Lemolo is made up of a boat anchor, euphemistically called a trolling rod, fitted with a reel loaded with heavy-test line. The heavy gear is not needed to handle the average 12-inch trout it catches, but to handle the trolling weights and keels and flashers on the terminal end of the line. Such gear is unsporting, and should be scorned; the fish has no chance against it, and, indeed, unless you hook a fish of trophy size, you won't even know it's there. However, a recent improvement in lake trolls (from Jim Teeny) has made lake trolling into a sporting proposition: the new troll has mylar and plastic propeller-like flashers instead of metal blades. It can be trolled behind an ultralight spinning rod or fly rod, and does not appreciably dampen the action of the rod or a fighting fish.

SPINNERS AND SPOONS

Spinning lures and spoons usually come from the manufacturer fitted with treble hooks. You'll hook more fish and lose fewer lures if you replace the treble hooks with single hooks. Mustad's No. 9510 has an open, ringed eye, and can be quickly clamped on a lure with needlenose pliers.

Often-used lures on the North Umpqua include spoons (the Stee-Lee and Krocodile and their clones), and weighted spinners. The more experienced hardware

fishermen do not cast-and-retrieve, but cast the lure out, allow it to bump down through a hole like a drift fishing rig, let it hang in the current for a few seconds at the end of the drift, and then retrieve it. Dyed-in-the-wool spinner fishermen expect to lose a lot of lures, and haunt garage sales and secondhand stores to keep their tackle boxes stocked with relatively cheap lures.

Effective lure colors include metallic green or blue; red, black, and white; natural metallic colors (chrome, brass, and copper); and fluorescent colors. When the water is low and clear, the more subdued color combinations — a red and white spoon, or red and white with a copper back, or black and white — are used. When the water is cold, or is beginning to show a little green, choose one of the bright colors or combinations of colors — metallic green or blue, red and chrome, red and brass, or chrome or brass. Fluorescent colors are reserved for the times when visibility in the water is reduced to a few feet, and chartreuse and other shades of green seem to be most effective in deep water.

PLUGGING

When the Hot Shot was a new thing, fishermen called it a "bug," and fishing with a bug was called bugging. Now, that type of fishing is called "plugging," and over a dozen different types of lures are commonly used; the most effective are generally conceded to be the Hot Shot, Wee Wart, and Hot 'N Tot.

"Plugging" is just another kind of trolling. The oarsman holds the boat back in the current, lets the plug out downstream of the boat, and the current works the plug. By far the greatest advantage of plug fishing (and the reason so many professional guides do it) is that an experienced fisherman on the oars can hook a tyro into a fish. Other advantages are that you spend more of a day fishing, and waste less of it casting and changing tackle; and since the more popular plugs are naturally buoyant, you break off less tackle on snags.

Luhr-Jensen has developed a Side Planer which allows a bank fisherman to work a Hot Shot through a fishing hole just like a boater would — but the combined cost of the plug and planer makes it a rigging you'd risk using only in places where you know there are no underwater obstructions.

Plugging does have its disadvantages. If there are many other boats on the river, you'll have drift fishermen rowing around you, casting into the spot you were setting up to fish, and catching the fish that should have been yours. Plugs also are not effective when the river is rising: rising water carries leaves and trash which foul a plug. A fouled plug won't run true, and even if it did, the fish wouldn't bite it.

Use light line; heavy line scares off leader-shy fish, and deadens the plug's action. Eight pound-test is usually adequate for summer fishing (6-pound is better if you feel confident using it), and 10-pound test is usually adequate for winter fishing. Slightly heavier line can be used when the water is off-color, or when the main thrust of a Chinook run — which usually carries the larger fish — is in the river.

Use a rod with a light tip, so you can tell when the plug is running properly by watching the action of the rod tip. The plug should run true; if it is out of tune and runs to one side or pops out of the water, it will not catch fish. The packaging the plug came in will have directions for tuning it.

Run the plug as close as possible to the boat. Twenty-five feet out is adequate if the water is a little off-color, and 35 to 40 feet out is far enough in clear water; any farther, and the plug becomes difficult for the oarsman to control.

Use large plugs and bright colors — silver with a red head, metallic green, or metallic blue — on dull days, or when the water is off-color. Use small plugs and dark or dull colors — white with a red or black head, or gold with a black back — when the water is clear. Use green or fluorescent colors and plugs with a rattle when the water is murky.

When fishing for fall Chinook, keep a close watch on the rod tip — sometimes the Chinook's take is so soft that the only evidence of the strike is that the rod tip quits working.

William Harvey and Lilly Weber on rocks at Tioga Falls (The Narrows) on the North Umpqua River, 1899. Douglas County Museum photo

Chapter 3

FLY PATTERNS

Ask any drift boating spin fisherman: all it takes to make a steelhead fly that works is to knot a piece of fluorescent yarn onto a bare hook (everyone has a favorite color, and they all work). The challenge becomes, then, not tying a fly that will catch a fish, but tying one that gives you a feeling of satisfaction when you complete it, confidence when you fish it, and pride when you land a fish on it. Resident trout, being more provincial than steelhead, are more comfortable with flies that look like the bugs they are accustomed to eating. The steelhead patterns described in this chapter aren't trendy or new or improved – but then, they don't have to be; they have been reliably hooking North Umpqua fish for decades, and will hook fish for you if you fish them correctly.

The author learned how to make the peacock herl chenille (described under Peacock & Alder) from Bob Houghton, an angling guide and fly tier from Eugene, Oregon. The Leech and Grasshopper patterns are the results of shortcuts on standard patterns the author developed while working as a commercial tier. The Grenade Fly has never held wide popularity because it is such a bear to cast – but, because of its effectiveness, it has a devoted following among the anglers who care more about hooking into fish than making graceful casts.

Except for a few special cases, like late season late evening hatches on the lakes, wet flies provide the best and the busiest trout fishing. Wet flies will, beyond any shadow of doubt, hook the largest fish. The patterns described below will catch fish in any situation you are likely to encounter in the North Umpqua drainage.

TYING MATERIALS AND TECHNIQUES

If you tie your own flies, you can do the things a commercial tier can't afford to spend time on, and end up with better quality flies (more durable and tied to catch fish instead of fishermen). To begin with, you can use more head cement: after you tie in the tail, wet the hook with head cement before you wrap on the body. This will bond the body of the fly to the hook, and make it hold up better against the ravages of a fish's teeth.

Use the softest, webbiest hackle you can find on your wet patterns. Commercial wet flies, and especially steelhead patterns, are usually hackled with rooster neck or saddle hackles; the same patterns tied with hen hackles will fish better: soft hackles take on water and sink faster, giving the fly more movement and life in the water.

When tying trout flies, pay close attention to proportions: unless the pattern requires variation, the tail of a fly should be no longer than the gap of the hook; the fly body should cover only the straight part of the shaft of the hook; the wing should be no longer than the body; and the head should be as small as practicable. Most steelhead patterns are attractors, and, though a properly proportioned attractor fly is much more attractive to the angler, it doesn't catch any more fish. A poorly tied steelhead fly is more likely to hook fish than a poorly tied trout fly.

The steelhead patterns shown in the color plate are tied on turned-up loop eye Atlantic salmon hooks, because sparse ties on up-eye hooks are more suited to the conditions when the North Umpqua summer steelhead run is in full flux – but that doesn't necessarily mean you should fish the year around with up-eye patterns. The eye of a hook tends to act as a diving plane, which means the current will push an up-eye hook toward the surface, and a down-eye hook toward the stream bottom. It follows that you should use down-eye, bushy ties during the early part of the season, when the fish are sluggish and won't move very far to take a fly, and save your low water ties for hot summer days, or early mornings (dawn to sunrise, when you are the first angler on the river, and the fish aren't yet line-shy), or for late in the summer when the river is low, clear, and slow. If in doubt, use flies on down-eye heavy wire hooks – Eagle Claw 1197 series or its equivalent.

You might consider tying a selection of weighted patterns to use when fishing swift water. Extremely heavy flies are difficult to cast, and making a poorly timed cast and burying a hook in your ear can weaken your resolve – but heavy flies do produce fish. The adage in drift fishing for steelhead is, if you're not losing tackle hanging up on the bottom, you're not doing it right. The same holds true of fly fishing: the fish hasn't changed its character simply because you're fishing fly fishing only water. Scraping a weighted fly along the bottom will catch fish, and drifting an unweighted fly through a hole several feet off the bottom will only catch those fish willing to move several feet to take a fly.

PATTERN SELECTION

Any selection of patterns will be somewhat arbitrary, and is bound to leave out somebody's pet killer pattern. The patterns listed below will all catch fish on the North Umpqua and its environs, are easy to tie, and are all durable if properly tied; each pattern pictured in the color plate has (P) after the name. The selection pictured in the color plate is sufficient to catch fish in all but

the rarest North Umpqua fishing situations.

The distinctions between steelhead flies and trout wet flies are more spurious than real when fishing the river, and they center more on size than pattern. Drift a steelhead fly through water that doesn't hold a steelhead but does hold trout, and you'll probably hook the trout; put a trout fly large enough in front of a steelhead's nose, and he'll probably take it.

Conditions are different on the lakes. However, some steelhead patterns (a Dark Spruce Fly or the variations on a Royal Coachman) are good trolling lures on some lakes, and, in a pinch, such black patterns as a Silver Hilton or Black Gordon can be used as leech imitators.

With few exceptions, the trout patterns listed aren't imitations of specific species of bugs, but impressionistic patterns that suggest a whole range of bugs a trout might invite home to lunch.

FLY PATTERNS

Cummings (P)
Hook: 2X strong, size 1/0 to 6
Thread: Black
Tail: None
Rib: Flat silver tinsel
Butt: Lemon yellow floss
Body: Burgundy wool
Hackle: Burgundy
Wing: Brown bucktail

According to Trey Combs *(Steelhead Fly Fishing and Flies)*, the Cummings was developed for fishing the North Umpqua by Ward Cummings and Clarence Gordon, during the 1930s. In all patterns calling for brown bucktail wings, the author substitutes the spiky brown fur from a badger's tail; badger tail is a slightly lighter brown, but has the same sort of translucent sparkle as polar bear fur, and makes a more attractive fly.

Black Gordon (P)
Hook: 2X strong, sizes 1/0 to 6
Thread: Black
Rib: Fine oval gold tinsel
Butt: Red wool
Body: Black wool
Hackle: Soft, webby black
Wing: Black bucktail

The present-day site of the Steamboat Inn is still named Gordon's Lodge on some maps; Clarence Gordon operated a lodge there under license from the U.S. Forest Service. According to all reports, he was an expert tier and fisherman, and the Black Gordon is one of the patterns he developed during the late thirties for fishing the North Umpqua.

Umpqua Special (P)
Hook: 2X strong, size 1 to 6
Thread: Black or red
Tail: Sparse red or orange (sometimes tied with no tail)
Rib: Silver tinsel
Butt: Yellow wool or floss
Body: Red wool
Hackle: Brown (sometimes tied with no hackle)
Wing: White and red bucktail. Tie in a white wing, then tie in a few strands of red or orange on each side.

As with so many of the standard patterns, the Umpqua Special was developed in the 1930s. Originally, the "Special" designated a fly tied with Jungle Cock cheeks; Jungle Cock eyes have become a rarity since the embargo on importation, but the name Umpqua Special has hung on, and is now used to describe the pattern tied without the Jungle Cock.

Black Woolly Worm
Hook: 2X long, size 4 to 8
Thread: Black
Tail: Sparse red hackle fibers
Rib: Flat silver tinsel
Hackle: Palmered grizzly
Body: Black Chenille

Another ancient pattern, simple to tie, easy to fish, and effective. The Woolly Worm is an effective lure for every species you can fish for in the fly fishing only section of the river.

Professor (P)
Hook: 2X strong, size 2 to 6
Thread: Black
Tail: Sparse red hackle fibers
Rib: Flat gold tinsel
Body: Lemon yellow floss
Hackle: Soft, webby brown
Wing: Rolled mallard flank feather, tied
    shorter than body

Sometimes tied using gray squirrel tail for a wing. Smaller sizes of the Professor and Kalama can be used for trout when yellow stoneflies are on the water.

Skunk (P)
Hook: 2X strong, size 1 to 8
Thread: Black
Tail: Red hackle fibers
Rib: Silver tinsel
Body: Black chenille
Hackle: Soft, webby black, tied sparse
Wing: White bucktail

The Skunk and its variations are probably the best-known of all steelhead patterns, and certainly among the most productive. Its more common variations are the Green-Butt Skunk, tied with a chartreuse butt; and the Red-Butt Skunk, tied with a red wool butt.

Al's Special (P)
Hook: 2X strong, sizes 2 to 6
Thread: Black
Tip: Fine oval silver tinsel
Tail: Sparse red hackle fibers
Rib: Medium oval silver tinsel
Body: Yellow chenille
Hackle: Webby red
Wing: White bucktail

Al Knudson moved to southern Oregon in 1929, and developed several fly patterns that have become standards. The Al's Special was developed in the early 1930s.

Van Luven (P)
Hook: 2X strong, size 1/0 to 6
Thread: Black
Tail: Red hackle fibers
Rib: Flat silver tinsel
Body: Red wool
Hackle: Soft, webby brown
Wing: White bucktail

The Van Luven is one of the few steelhead flies that imitates something in nature — fresh roe. If you can't decide which pattern suits the conditions, play it safe and tie on a Van Luven. A logger of the author's acquaintance (who likes to fly fish for the Chinook on the North Umpqua) fishes a Van Luven — and Chinook are a difficult fish to connect with on a fly rod. The Van Luven and Thor can be fished interchangeably — the only difference is the color of the tail.

Kalama (P)
Hook: 2X strong, size 2 to 6
Thread: Black
Tail: Sparse red hackle fibers
Hackle: Badger saddle, palmered
Body: Lemon yellow floss or wool
Wing: White bucktail

The Kalama is a good pattern to fish early in the morning, late in the evening, and on dark days.

Silver Hilton (P)
Hook: 2X strong, sizes 1 to 6
Thread: Black
Tail: A few fibers from a mallard
  flank feather
Rib: Flat silver tinsel
Body: Black chenille or (for
  low water ties on light
  wire hooks) black wool
Hackle: Soft, webby grizzly
Wing: Grizzly hackle tips, tied
  back-to-back

A northern California pattern that works well on the North Umpqua when the water and weather are clear. The most often fished size is a No. 4; larger sizes are fished by anglers who particularly like the pattern, and hate to change to a red pattern when the water goes off color. Move down to a size 6 for late season, late evening fishing.

Purple Peril (P)
Hook: 2X strong, size 1/0 to 6
Thread: Black or purple
Tip: Silver tinsel
Tail: Purple Hackle fibers, sparse
Rib: Fine silver tinsel
Body: Purple Floss or wool
Hackle: Purple
Wing: Brown Bucktail

Pattern developed by Ken MacLeod in the 1950s. Here's what Dennis Brandsma, an excellent steelhead fisherman, has to say about the Purple Peril: "I don't start fishing with a purple fly, but if the fish are striking short on a black fly − a Silver Hilton or a Skunk − I'll switch to a Purple Peril, because they'll take it solidly."

Carson Coachman (P)
Hook: 2X strong, size 8 and 10
Thread: Black
Tail: Sparse red hackle fibers
Butt: Peacock herl chenille
Body: Red floss
Shoulder: Peacock herl
Hackle: Coachman red
*Wing: Red and white calf tail: bottom one-
    third white, center one-third red, top
    one-third white.*

Smaller sizes are a good brook trout lure when trolled in lakes, and when fished in broken water and pocket water on the river; use the larger sizes for steelhead.

Poodle Dog (P)
Hook: 2X strong, size 1 to 6 (steelhead)
*   and 8 to 12 (trout)*
Thread: Black
Tail: Red hackle fibers
Butt: Peacock herl chenille,
*   two turns (see Peacock*
*   & Alder, below)*
Body: Flat silver tinsel
Shoulder: Peacock herl, two turns
Hackle: White
Wing: White bucktail

Originated in the 1950s for fishing the Stillaguamish River. A variation of a Royal Coachman that uses tinsel instead of red floss for the body. Variations of the Poodle Dog are the author's favorite attractor patterns: Var. No. 1 − as above, but hackled with one turn of partridge breast feather. Var No. 2 − as in Var. No. 1, but with a gold tinsel body and wing made from a rolled mottled brown grouse feather.

Dark Spruce Fly (P)
Hook: 2X long, size 6 or 8
Thread: Black
Tail: A few peacock sword fibers, or, If you
don't have the sword, herl fibers clipped
to length.
Body: Rear half — red floss
Front half — peacock
herl chenille (see Peacock & Alder)
Hackle: Soft, webby furnace
Wings: Furnace hackle tips tied
back-to-back

The Dark Spruce is a pretty pattern that will catch river trout, steelhead, and (when trolled) lake brown and rainbow trout. The original Spruce Fly was tied with badger hackle and wings, but the furnace works better on the North Umpqua. This is not a durable fly, and there is nothing you can do to make it durable, but it is a killer.

Red Ant (P)
Hook: 2X strong, size 6 to 12
Thread: Black or red
Tip: Silver tinsel
Tail: Red hackle fibers
Butt: Peacock herl chenille (see
Peacock & Alder below) or a single
strand of ostrich herl
Rib: Fine gold tinsel
Body: Red floss
Hackle: Brown
Wing: Brown calf tail, tied sparse,
at about a 25- to 30-degree
angle from the hook

As you see from the description of the tie, the Red Ant used on the North Umpqua is different from the original Rogue River Red Ant. A Rogue River Red Ant is tied on a double hook, without a tip, without hackle, and with divided wings. Double-hook, divided wing patterns can be fished on the North Umpqua, but are frustrating, because they are designed to be trolled downstream of a drift boat. The double hooks are awkward to cast, and, since most tiers tie the split wings too long, the wings usually tangle around the hook. The pattern as described above is easy to tie, easy to fish, and productive.

Mormon Girl (P)
Hook: 2X strong, size 4 to 10
Thread: Black
Tail: None
Butt: Red Floss
Body: Yellow Floss
Hackle: Palmered grizzly
Wing: Rolled mallard flank feather

The Mormon Girl is a western cutthroat pattern, but it also works to startling effect on brook and rainbow trout on the upper river and its tributaries.

Peacock & Alder (P)
Hook: 2X strong, sizes 4 and 6
  (steelhead), and 10, 12, and
  14 (trout)
Thread: Black
Tail: None
Body: Peacock herl
Hackle: A soft, mottled brown
  feather from the wing of a
  pheasant or partridge, tied
  in by the tip

A variation on an ancient trout pattern. When tying the body, tie in a 6-inch piece of tying thread and (depending on hook size), 6 or more peacock herl strands by the tips; twist the peacock herl strands and thread together clockwise to form a chenille, and wrap the chenille forward and tie it off. Single strands of peacock herl are fragile; twisting several into a chenille, as described, makes a body that tapers nicely to the head and won't fall apart the first time a brown trout chews on it. Clearwater River brook trout like it better if tied weighted.

Brown Stone
Hook: Mustad 94831, size 10
  or 12
Thread: Orange
Hackle: Grizzly rooster hackle,
  palmered
Body: Beige wool
Wing: Sparse blonde elk body
  hair

The Brown Stone is a productive trout pattern in small streams and the river and late in the season (August to October).

Grenade Fly (P)

Hook: Down-eye 3X or 4X long,
* size 4, 6, or 8*
Underbody: Lead fuse wire wrapped up
* the hook, then well-coated with head*
* cement. Use 3 amp wire for size 4, 2 amp*
* wire for size 6, and 1 amp wire for size 8.*
Thread: Fluorescent orange size A
Tail: Black marabou extending back
* the length of the gap of*
* the hook*
Hackle: Long, webby brown, palmered
Body: Black chenille

After the tie is completed, bend the front one third of the hook down about 45 degrees toward the point. The grenade fly was originated by Galand Haas and Phil Pirone for use on the Deschutes River, but has been cloned, renamed, and claimed as original by several well-known angling writers. It is a consistently productive trout and steelhead pattern on the North Umpqua. The color makes it highly visible, the weight gets it down in moving water, and the bend in the hook makes it tumble down through the drift in semblance of the gymnastics of a stonefly nymph dislodged from its rock and trying to regain its balance. Size 4 is the most productive size on the fast-flowing parts of the river; go to a size 6 or 8 in the slower stretches where the fish has more time to look at the fly before he decides whether he wants to take it. The name Grenade Fly is a reference to the splash this heavily weighted fly makes when it hits the water. Grenade also gives you a good idea of what to expect if you make a miscast and wallop yourself in the back of the head with such a heavily weighted pattern.

Leech (Olive or Black)

Hook: Down eye 2X long, size 6 to 10
Thread: Black
Tail, Body, and Wing: Marabou
* — olive green or black*

Tie the entire fly from one marabou feather. Don't cut the feather until the body of the fly is completed. Tie in the tip of the feather to make a tail about twice as long as the gap of the hook. Wrap the thread forward. Twist the marabou clockwise to make a rope, and wrap it forward and tie it off. Clip off the remainder of the feather, pull off a section of the down and tie it in as a wing; clip the wing to a length of about one third the length of the body.

The Leech is a productive fly in the lakes of the North Umpqua. The best ways to fish the fly are (1) trolled dead slow on a sink-tip line, parallel to the shore along steep drop-offs, with action imparted to the fly by twitching the rod tip; or (2) casting with a sink-tip along a steep drop-off, allowing the fly to sink to the limits of the line, and retrieving in short, quick twitches.

The best color is the one that catches fish: carry black and olive, begin fishing with the olive, and if it doesn't work, switch to the black.

Adams Wet (P)
Hook: Down eye, heavy wire,
  size 10 to 16
Thread: Black
Tail: Very sparse mixed coachman
  red and grizzly hackle
  fibers; no tail on size
  No. 14 and No. 16
Body: Grey wool or dubbed
  mole belly fur.
Hackle: Very sparse mixed coachman
  red and grizzly; no
  hackle on sizes 14 and 16.
Wing: Grizzly hackle tips tied
  spent back-to-back

If you are fishing a lake during a hatch, can see fish rising all around you, but aren't getting strikes on dry flies, try fishing two wet flies at a time: the Adams Wet on a dropper, and a Mosquito (described below) on the tippet. Keep the flies wet, so they sink as soon as your cast settles, and begin retrieving in short jerks as soon as they touch the water.

Mosquito Larva (P)
Hook: Mustad 94840, size 10
  to 20
Thread: Black
Body: Stripped grizzly quill, tied
  in by the tip, so it tapers
  larger toward the head.
Hackle: Sparse grizzly

The larger sizes resemble several larvae found crawling around under the rocks in the river, and sizes 18 and 20 imitate the mosquito wigglers squirming around in backwaters of the high lakes.

Olive Mayfly Nymph
Hook: Mustad 94831, size 10
  and 12
Body: Olive green dubbing, tied
  skinny, tapered larger
  toward the head.
Hackle: Grizzly rooster hackle, one turn

A pattern effective throughout the river through the first half of the summer.

Olive Caddis (P)
Hook: Down eye heavy wire,
size 10 to 16
Thread: Black
Rib: Ginger hackle palmered,
then clipped short
Body: Olive dubbing, tapered
larger toward the head
Wing: Deer body hair. When the
wing is tied on, the deer
hair will flare; work a little
more dubbing onto the thread,
and wrap the dubbing around
the fly at the base of the
wing to pull the wing in tight
against the body, and tie
the thread off.

The development of this particular tying fillip — using dubbing to pad the tying thread and stop deer hair from flaring — has been attributed to Bob Borden.

This is a wet fly, but if you dress the deer hair wing, it can be fished dry: the body will sink and the wing will hold the fly on the surface. It sounds odd, but the fish like it.

Effective during the first half of the summer; after the first of August, replace the Olive Caddis with a Brown Stone.

Grasshopper (P)
Hook: Mustad 94831, size 6
to 10
Thread: Primrose
Tail: Sparse red dry hackle
fibers
Body: Yellow floss
Wing: Mottled turkey quill
section, lacquered
Head: Spun deer body hair, clipped
to roughly the shape of a
grasshopper's head and thorax.
Leave a few long hairs
trailing behind the head
to look like legs.

A pattern the author evolved over the last dozen years or so; it fishes as well as any other grasshopper, but is simpler and quicker to tie. Grasshoppers, Muddlers, and other patterns dressed heavily with deer body hair can also be used as steelhead flies: when you know there's a fish there, and you know you're putting a fly over him, but he just won't strike, floating a dry fly by that sputters and buzzes and kicks up a ruckus on the surface will sometimes irritate the fish into striking.

Light Cahill (P)
Hook: Down eye, heavy wire,
*   size 10 to 16*
Thread: Tan or black
Tail: None
Body: Tan dubbing
Wing: Rolled wood duck or
*   mallard flank feather*
Hackle: A few turns of light
*   ginger or white rooster*
*   hackle*

On the river, the larger sizes seem to work best; use smaller sizes on lakes.

Crane Fly (P)
Hook: Mustad 94831, size 6
*   to 10*
Thread: Orange
Body: Primrose floss
Hackle: One turn of grizzly
*   rooster hackle*
Wings: Grizzly hackle tips, tied
*   at a 45-degree angle up and*
*   back from the body*

This is an effective late evening pattern along the verges of the high lakes, and in the deeper, slower holes of the river. Dress it with floatant, and it will ride in the surface film; retrieve it in short, erratic twitches. A slight backward bend in the shank of the hook (see color plate) makes the fly look better, but the fish probably won't notice one way or the other.

Dry Flies

Only rarely is precise matching of the hatch necessary on the North Umpqua. The single possible exception is the early stonefly hatch. Large golden olive-to-orange stoneflies begin hatching out on the North Umpqua at about the same time the rhododendrons begin blooming. They hatch on through until the blackberries are ripe, and may continue hatching sporadically through the remainder of the summer.

However, matching the hatch, even when the stonefly hatch is in full flux, is not really necessary, since other patterns — particularly stonefly nymphs — will catch fish during the stonefly hatch. Rainbow and brook trout are finned opossums: they will humbly and gratefully eat whatever fare you present to them and are seldom overcritical of your presentation. Brown trout can be choosy, but the habitat conspires against them on the North Umpqua.

When a hatch is coming off one of the lakes, there will invariably be a breeze riffling the surface, which distorts the fish's view of the fly. Impressionistic patterns — Light Cahill, Adams, Olive Quill, Mosquito, or one of the caddises dressed with floatant — will prove satisfactory. On Lemolo during the middle of the summer, for example, 2 or 3 bugs will be hatching off all day, but fishing dry flies (even if they precisely match the hatch) is a waste of time. However, when the shadows lengthen, the late afternoon chill sets in, and a light breeze springs up, the fish will begin feeding on the surface. Let your boat drift, and cast out a No. 16 or No. 18 Adams or Mosquito, and the action will be sure and steady; you'll have fish on almost every cast. Then, when the sun drops behind the hill, and the breeze dies, the bugs are still hatching, but the fish quit feeding on the surface.

When a hatch is coming off the river, the current is moving the bugs fast enough that the trout don't have much opportunity to get critical — they have only a few seconds to grab what's offered — so matching the size and approximating the color of the naturals will usually suffice.

The following list of dry flies is ranked by usefulness — the essential patterns are at the top of the list, and the most useful sizes are listed first; the nice-to-have-along patterns are at the bottom of the list. You will have every usual dry fly fishing situation in the North Umpqua corridor covered if you carry all the patterns listed below.

Mosquito — 18, 16, 10. Size 18 and 16 Mosquitoes are the dry flies of choice for late evening lake fishing. If the early season pale blue mayflies are hatching off, and you don't have an Adams in in your fly box, a size 10 Mosquito will usually work. A size 10 Mosquito is a good pattern to use when you are dry fly fishing downstream in the smaller creeks, just hoping to startle a fish into rising by offering him something that looks good to eat.

Adams — 16, 10. Occasionally, especially after Labor Day, high lakes fish will prefer an Adams to a Mosquito. Early in the year a large blue mayfly (with brown-mottled transparent wings) will hatch off sporadically above the 4,000-foot level; one would think a Blue Dun would be the fly to use, but, in the author's experience, the fish prefer an Adams.

Light Cahill — 16, 12. On the lower river (downstream from Upper Island hole), from about the fourth of July through the end of the season, hatches come off the deep, slow runs of the river. Sometime the fish are slurping a bug so small it can't be imitated with a fly; sometimes they're feeding on a tiny lemon yellow stone, and can be taken with a size 16 Light Cahill. The size 16 will also take fish from the high lakes when any of several light greenish, yellowish, and tan insects are hatching. When the yellow and orange stoneflies are hatching, a size 12 Light Cahill will occasionally produce fish.

Grasshopper — 12, 10, 6. However, the Grasshopper pattern pictured in the color plate works better. If the orange stones are hatching, use a size 10; if yellow stones are hatching, use size 12. Load the fly with floatant, cast it across-current out on a long, fine leader, and let it it drag along the surface until it hangs downstream from you; twitch the tip of your rod every second or so, and when the fly hangs below you, retrieve it in short twitches. The dragging and twitching action resembles the spluttering and buzzing commotion the adult fly makes depositing its eggs. The size 6 Grasshopper can also be fished as a natural — as a search pattern on streams, and along grassy shorelines of lakes where terrestrials fall into the water.

Kolzer Dark Caddis — 4, 6, and 8. When the stoneflies are on water that moves slow enough, the fish can take their time looking a fly over, Kolzer Dark Caddis will outfish the Grasshopper; because the Grasshopper is so hard to sink, it is a good choice for fishing pockets in whitewater.

Black Gnat — 20, 14. A size 20 Black Gnat is a frustration fly: when the no-see-ums are making you miserable in the high country, tie it on, and you'll probably catch fish. A size 14 is a good search pattern on smaller streams during the hot part of summer.

Chapter 4

GAMEFISH of the NORTH UMPQUA

The gamefish commonly caught in the North Umpqua region include winter Chinook salmon, spring Chinook salmon, coho (silver) salmon, winter steelhead trout, summer steelhead trout, rainbow trout, cutthroat trout, sea-run cutthroat trout, brown trout, and brook trout. Incidental catches include whitefish and carp in the river, and kokanee (small landlocked salmon) in Hemlock Lake.

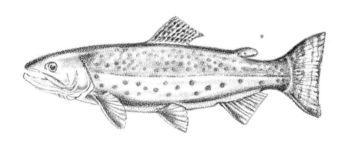

Brook Trout

(Salvelinus fontinalis)

The brook trout is a native of the upper East Coast of the United States and southern Canada, brought to the west coast in the 1920s and 1930s.

Brook trout are the brightest colored of the fishes in the North Umpqua region, typically having a dark olive, almost black back, fading off into muddy gray sides and a bright orange belly. The back is salted with vermiculations (wormlike markings), and the sides are speckled with bright red and yellow spots surrounded by a soft gray-blue halo. The pectoral, ventral, and anal fins have a white leading edge, backed by a black stripe that fades off into reddish orange and yellow. The tail fin (as with other chars) is forked.

Brook trout may be found in the Clearwater River, in all the North Umpqua reservoirs from Toketee upstream, occasionally in the North Umpqua River itself, in Lake Creek upstream of Lemolo, and in Calamut, Fuller, Lucile, Maidu, and Skipper Lakes.

They are more of a cold water fish than either brown or rainbow trout, so you are more likely to catch them early in the season and very late in the season. In lakes, you are more likely to catch brookies in deeper water, where the temperatures are lowest. In streams, like Lake Creek, they seem to favor the slower-flowing runs and such cover as undercut banks and logs.

Brookies are aggressive feeders, and aren't particularly choosy. They'll take whatever bait is offered; small spinners, especially copper- or brass-colored, work well in most of the small streams (except the Clearwater River). They have a reputation for liking brightly colored flies, but on the North Umpqua, patterns like the Light Cahill, Black Gnat, and Peacock & Alder seem to produce more fish.

Large brook trout are sometimes called squaretails because the fork in their tails becomes less pronounced. A good average brookie in the North Umpqua corridor will be 6 or 7 inches long, and you may occasionally catch a squaretail in one of the reservoirs.

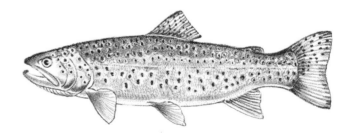

Brown Trout (Loch Leven Trout, German Brown)
(Salmo trutta)

Brown trout are not native to North America; early stocking strains in the western United States came from Germany or from Scotland's Loch Leven — hence the nicknames. The brown's tolerance of poor habitat makes it a popular fish on the North Umpqua: Lemolo Reservoir (for example) is very nearly barren — there are few nutrients in the water, and little aquatic vegetation — and Lemolo's browns are consistently larger than its rainbows.

Very few brown trout caught along the North Umpqua are likely to be brown; a typical North Umpqua brown will have an olive green back shading into muddy yellow on the sides. Its back will be sprinkled with black spots, and on its sides, the black spots will be interspersed with red spots surrounded by a yellow or light-blue halo.

Along the North Umpqua Corridor, brown trout can be found in Bridge Prairie Reservoir, Lemolo No. 1 and No. 2 Forebays, Lemolo Reservoir, Soda Springs Reservoir, Toketee Reservoir, Lake Creek, and occasionally in the river itself in the runs between reservoirs and upstream of Boulder Flat.

North Umpqua browns retain all their race's fabled ability to frustrate anglers: in some places at some times, they readily take any lure from earthworms to dry flies; at other times, when there are two or three life stages of half a dozen different bugs on the water, the trout will be taking only one life stage of one species of bug, and the angler has to figure out which one. The only statements that can safely be made about brown trout angling on the North Umpqua are that most are caught by fly fishermen, but the largest ones (over 5 pounds) are usually caught in Lemolo Reservoir, and are usually caught by trollers.

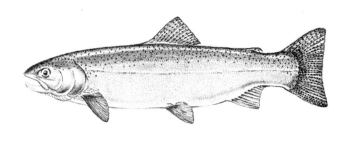

Rainbow Trout (Redsides, Steelhead)
(Salmo gairdneri)

The North Umpqua has large populations of rainbow trout and their seagoing brothers, summer and winter steelhead. Most of the resident rainbow are hatchery stock — a chunky, deep-bodied race with a dark olive back, a pinkish rainbow stripe along each side that gives it its name, silver sides that fade into a white belly, and speckled with small dark spots. Trout released from the hatchery will be about 8 inches long, and holdover fish (hatchery fish that don't die or get caught) will grow to 10 or 11 inches by their second season in the river. Larger fish that have been in the river longer will begin to take

on more of the characteristics of a wild fish — brighter coloring, firmer, pinker flesh, and more strength and stamina when fighting.

Some anglers have trouble telling the difference between downstream migrant smolts and rainbow trout. On the North Umpqua, fin clips help: the 45,000 to 50,000 catchable rainbow dumped into the river every year are not fin-clipped, but every steelhead and salmon smolt released from the Rock Creek Hatchery will have some combination of fin and maxillary clips. Anglers still take a few smolts, but the late May season opening date and 8 inch minimum size limit are both calculated to reduce the problem. According to Department of Fish & Wildlife figures, the "trout" catch on the North Umpqua averages 97% hatchery rainbow, 1% native trout, and 2% downstream migrant smolts.

A fresh steelhead — that is, one recently returned from salt water — will be colored like a river rainbow, except that it is not likely to have a rainbow stripe down its lateral line. Once it is acclimated to the river, the red stripe will begin to show up along its sides, and will become a deep muddy crimson by the time the fish is ready to spawn. A fish that has spawned (termed a *runback*, *spawner*, or *snake* by anglers) will be gaunt, show little fight when hooked, and its belly will have turned a sooty gray color. Such fish should be returned to the river to get the chance to live and spawn again.

Summer steelhead will average 7 to 9 pounds each, and winter steelhead will average a few pounds heavier; fish weighing in excess of 15 pounds are common, and the author has seen fish as large as 26 pounds taken from the lower river.

The fish fresh from the ocean is the best for eating; a fish showing a red stripe down its side will still be acceptable table fare so long as its sides and belly are bright and silvery. When the red stripe has become pronounced, and the sides and belly are losing their luster, the fish is no longer fit to eat.

Over the last 15 years, the North Umpqua summer steelhead run has averaged 9,900 fish, and the winter run (which is not supplemented by hatchery fish) has averaged 7,300 fish. Currently, about 23,000 fish per year cross the fish ladder at Winchester; anglers catch about 2 of every 3 summer fish, and one of 5 winter fish; the average escapement to spawn is about 5900 winter fish and 5200 summer fish. Summer steelhead begin to show up in the lower end of the North Umpqua around the end of May. They are in the river in good numbers by the middle of June, usually scattered throughout the river from Soda Springs to Glide by the middle of July, and spawning in the autumn. Winter Steelhead first show up in the river around Christmas, and are scattered throughout the river by the middle of January, and spawn from February to April.

There is no passage around Soda Springs Dam, and therefore no anadromous fish above Soda Springs.

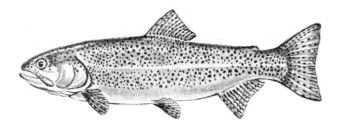

Cutthroat Trout
(Black Spotted Trout, Cutt, Harvest Trout)
(Salmo clarki)

There is no hatchery replenishment of cutthroat trout in the North Umpqua, so, while you might catch a cutthroat anywhere in the North Umpqua drainage — mostly in the smaller tributary creeks — their total numbers are small. The Department of Fish & Wildlife doesn't help the cutthroat because cutthroat are not what they call a "target fishery," and because cutthroat are more difficult to raise in a hatchery — rainbow are hardier under captive conditions, and are more prolific spawners.

Being a poor relation (so to speak) does have its benefits, though: having to survive without artificial help has made them more pugnacious than hatchery rainbow — occasionally you'll think you've hooked a 10-inch rainbow, only to discover when you land it that it's a 7-inch cutt. In areas where cutts and rainbows look much alike, two distinguishing characteristics help you tell which is which. The red slash on the cutthroat's underjaw that gives it its name, and the length of its mouth (a cutthroat's mouth extends back past its eye, and a rainbow's mouth does not). North Umpqua cutthroat show the usual family resemblance to rainbows, but are much brighter colored: the underjaw slash is bright, blood red, the fins all have a reddish tinge, and the black spots that give it one of its nicknames are much more sharply defined than the spots on a rainbow.

The North Umpqua also supports a small population of sea-run cutthroat. The sea-run cutts will average 15 or 16 inches long, and their nickname — harvest trout — tells you when they are in the river. Sea-run cutts aren't likely to be caught above Whistler's Bend, and most are caught accidentally by anglers prospecting for an early winter-run steelhead. The sea-run cutthroat population has fluctuated wildly over the last several decades; since the few years hatchery fish returned were also low-return years, it is possible that some of the fluctuation is due to fish straying back and forth between the north and south forks at the end of their migration. However,

the run has gotten progressively smaller over the past decade, and may die out altogether without help.

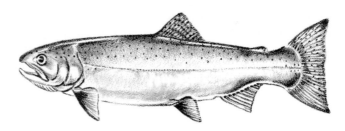

Coho Salmon (Silversides, Silver Salmon)
(Oncorhynchus kisutch)

While sea-run rainbow and cutthroat trout may migrate back to salt water and return to spawn more than one time, Pacific salmon die after spawning.

North Umpqua coho will average about the same size as summer steelhead. Coho and steelhead occasionally fight the same sort of battle when hooked, with considerable jumping and aerial acrobatics. Sometimes, when fresh from the ocean, they look enough alike to cause confusion — but coho and steelhead are easily distinguishable. Steelhead have a white mouth, and coho have a black mouth with a white gum line. Steelhead have 12 or fewer anal fin rays; salmon have more than 12. Once acclimated to the river, the coho begins to darken; when its skin has lost its silvery color, the flesh is no longer fit to eat.

Most of the coho end their upstream migration at the hatchery at Rock Creek, and any caught upstream of the hatchery are likely to be wild fish. Before 1981, the coho in the North Umpqua were an entirely wild run. The run began declining in the 1960s, and by the late 1970s, fewer than 500 fish per year were counted crossing Winchester Dam. A hatchery program was started, and by 1985, the average yearly return had climbed to just over 3,800 fish. Coho usually begin showing up in the lower end of the river in October and are spawning by Christmas.

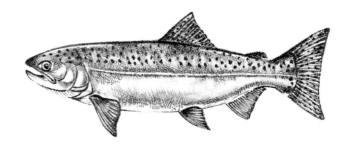

Chinook Salmon
(Oncorhynchus tshawytscha)

36

The North Umpqua has two Chinook runs: the fall run starts in the autumn, a month or so before Thanksgiving, and the spring run usually begins showing up about the middle of May. Although the Chinook has several nicknames elsewhere — blackmouth, king, and tyee — the only nickname in common use on the North Umpqua is springer, used to describe a spring-run fish.

Chinook, as one of their nicknames implies, have an entirely black mouth — but you don't have to see a Chinook's mouth to identify him. Where steelhead and coho are given to frantic, sizzling surface runs and aerial acrobatics, a Chinook is a bulldog fighter who holds stubbornly to the bottom of the hole, and may never be seen by the angler until it is tired out and almost ready to come to net. Occasionally, an angler who thinks he has hung up on a submerged log all of a sudden feels the log start to move, and discovers he's hooked into a large Chinook.

Spring and fall run fish both average about the same size; most fish caught will run 12 to 14 pounds, but fish larger than 20 pounds are not uncommon, and fish over 30 pounds are occasionally heard of. Most of the exceptionally large fish landed by sport fishermen — the ones that weigh in excess of 35 pounds — are caught in the ocean or tidewater. There simply is not enough room to fight such a large fish in a fast-flowing river like the North Umpqua, and the angler who hooks into such a fish will probably break it off.

The Life Cycle of Anadromous Fishes

An anadromous fish is one which is spawned in fresh water, migrates downstream to live a part of its life in salt water, and returns to fresh water to spawn and complete the cycle. Salmonid fishes — salmon, trout, and chars — can all tolerate a salt water environment, but do not all migrate to the ocean. Not all races of cutthroat trout migrate to salt water; those which do remain near the river mouth and do not venture out into the open sea. Steelhead (seagoing rainbow trout), like salmon, are truly pelagic — that is, once they exit the river they head for the open sea — and virtually nothing is known about what happens to them during their stay in salt water.

Much is made of an anadromous fish's unerring ability to return to the same stream, and sometimes the same gravel bar, where it was spawned; this ability is not yet completely understood, but it is known that the ability is not infallible, and fish do occasionally stray and spawn in different rivers. Steelhead and sea-run cutthroat sometimes stray back and forth from the north and south forks of the Umpqua. Private commercial hatcheries sometimes add dyes and scents to the water before releasing smolts, then use the same combinations of dye and scent to attract returning fish to their catch tanks.

Adult fish spawn in gravel beds, called redds. For the spawn to be successful, the gravel beds must be made up of pea- to cobble-sized wash gravel. Siltation — fine silt and mud washing in and filling the spaces between rocks — has destroyed much spawning habitat in recent decades. The most usual cause of siltation is the erosion that occurs after the clearcutting of timber.

By the time it is ripe for spawning, as much as a third of the fish's body weight may be made up of reproductive tissue (the part of the fish's body that produces eggs or milt). Female fish (called hens) are, on the average, larger than male fish (called bucks). After the male and female fish are paired and ready to spawn, the female digs a trench in the gravel, using her body like a bulldozer blade; the male moves up alongside her, and both hover over the trench. The eggs and sperm are squirted into the trench together, and the hen covers the fertilized eggs with gravel.

The fish does not break out of the egg to hatch, like a chicken; the newly hatched fish, or alevin, has the egg attached to its abdomen, and gradual absorption of the egg provides the alevin with food to survive on while it learns how to eat.

The alevin spends the first few months of its life hidden in the gravel of the streambed; when it can swim well enough to avoid predators, it emerges from the gravel and swims free in the river.

After a year (or sometimes two years) of growth in the river, the smolt — which is usually 5 or 6 inches long — begins its migration downstream to the ocean. The downstream migration usually occurs in the springtime.

Fish scales have annular rings, like trees; by "reading" the rings on a scale under a microscope, a biologist can tell how many years a returning adult fish has spent in salt water, and the number of years the fish spent in salt water is used as a shorthand to describe the fish — thus a "one salt" has spent a year in the ocean, a "two salt" two years, and so forth. Some races of some species spend as much as 4 years in salt water, but most fish returning to the North Umpqua to spawn are one salt or two salt fish.

Adults returning to spawn may travel more than 10 miles upstream per day, and may linger at the upper end of the migration for 2 months or more before spawning. The rate of travel is largely determined by water conditions: if the water is warm and low, the fish may not move at all. A freshet may cause the fish to sprint upstream.

Chinook and coho begin to deteriorate as soon as they enter fresh water. By the time they spawn, their skin will have turned dark purple or black, and their upper bodies will be covered with white degenerative sores. Shortly after spawning, Pacific salmon die.

Steelhead and cutthroat, on the other hand, do not markedly deteriorate in fresh water; they take on a silvery coloration in salt water, revert to their normal coloration in fresh water, and darken considerably during and after the spawn – but their changes in color are a result of ripening to spawn, and of the stresses of spawning. Although many sea-run trout will die from stress-related problems after spawning, their death is not inevitable like a salmon's; many live to spawn more than once.

A pair of spawning fish may deposit thousands of fertile eggs in the gravel. Some do not hatch. Of those that hatch, most fall victim to predation or disease. On the average, the end product of all those thousands of eggs – if nature is not interfered with – is two more spawning adult fish.

FIN CLIPS AND TAGS

As noted earlier in this chapter, the 45,000 or so trout released into the North Umpqua each year are not fin-clipped; clipping them would be a great deal of work and would serve no useful purpose.

However, every anadromous fish that leaves the hatchery will either have a fin or maxillary bone clip – and when the fish returns to the hatchery, the clips can tell a biologist much about the fish's early life.

The amount of information any combination of fin clips can convey is limited, but high-tech has come to the aid of fisheries biologists in the form of a small metal pin – barely large enough to be seen with the naked eye, but capable of carrying an astounding amount of information. The pin, injected into the nose of smolts before release, is made of ferrous metal so it can be located by a metal detector and retrieved with a magnet, and coated with stainless steel to be non-corrosible. After retrieval, the information carried by the pin is read under a microscope. At the Rock Creek Hatchery, smolts injected with the metal pin have an adipose fin clip. Smolts released in the summer of 1987 illustrate the range of information the pin can carry. The fish were fed different diet formulas, and released from the hatchery ponds into the river at varying ages. By reading the pins when the fish return to the hatchery, the technicians can tell which group a particular fish came from, and may be able to tell which combination of diet and release age yields the largest fish return.

This wrinkled dorsal fin hatchery-origin, summer run steelhead took a fly presented with a shooting head system for long distance fly casting. Deke Meyer photo

NORTH UMPQUA RIVER MAPS

SCALE 1:62 500

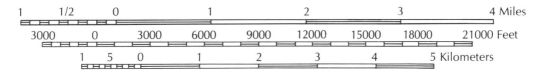

KEY MAP

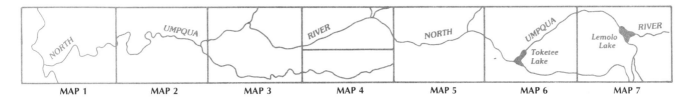

MAP 1   MAP 2   MAP 3   MAP 4   MAP 5   MAP 6   MAP 7

LEGEND

Interstate Highway

U.S. Highway

State Highway

Nat. Forest Primary Rd

Paved or Hard Surface Rd

Gravel Road, Dirt Road

Railroad

Trail

Camping

Picnicking

Boat Ramp

Fishing Access

Trailer

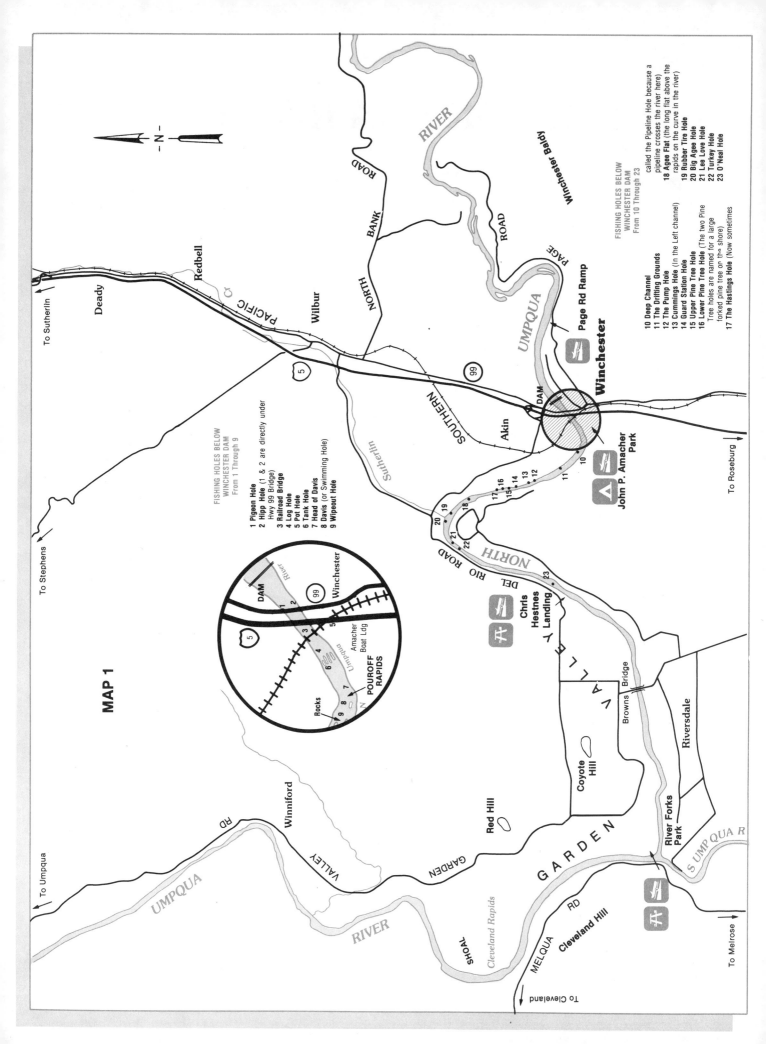

MAP 1

FISHING HOLES BELOW WINCHESTER DAM
From 1 Through 9

1 Pigeon Hole
2 Hipp Hole (1 & 2 are directly under Hwy 99 Bridge)
3 Railroad Bridge
4 Log Hole
5 Pot Hole
6 Tank Hole
7 Head of Davis
8 Davis (or Swimming Hole)
9 Wipeout Hole

FISHING HOLES BELOW WINCHESTER DAM
From 10 Through 23

10 Deep Channel
11 The Drifting Grounds
12 The Pump Hole
13 Cummings Hole (In the Left channel)
14 Guard Station Hole
15 Upper Pine Tree Hole
16 Lower Pine Tree Hole (The two Pine Tree holes are named for a large forked pine tree on the shore)
17 The Hastings Hole (Now sometimes called the Pipeline Hole because a pipeline crosses the river here)
18 Agee Flat (the long flat above the rapids on the curve in the river)
19 Rubber Tire Hole
20 Big Agee Hole
21 Lee Love Hole
22 Turkey Hole
23 O'Neal Hole

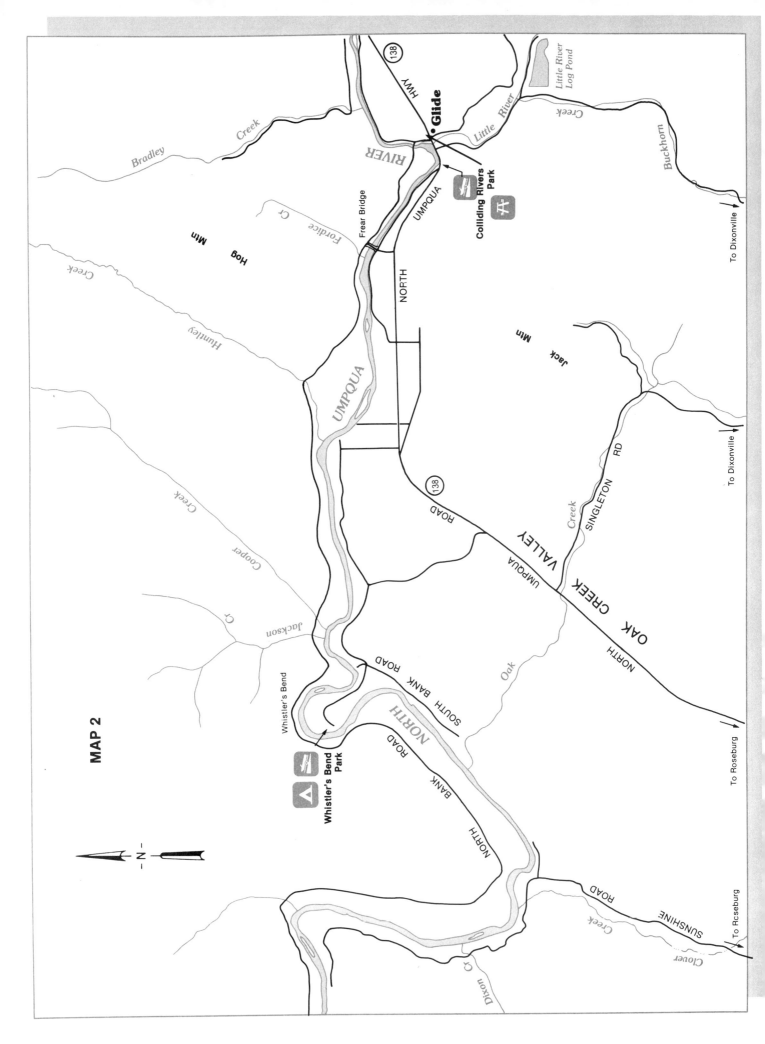

MAP 2

Glide

138 HWY

Little River Log Pond

Little River

Creek

Buckhorn

To Dixonville

Colliding Rivers Park

Bradley Creek

RIVER

NORTH UMPQUA

Frear Bridge

Hog Mtn

Fordice Cr

Jack Mtn

Creek

To Dixonville

Creek

Huntley

UMPQUA

138 ROAD

SINGLETON RD

UMPQUA VALLEY

OAK CREEK VALLEY

NORTH

Creek

Cooper

Oak

To Roseburg

Cr

Jackson

SOUTH BANK ROAD

Whistler's Bend

NORTH BANK ROAD

Whistler's Bend Park

Creek

SUNSHINE ROAD

To Roseburg

Clover Creek

Dixon Cr

N

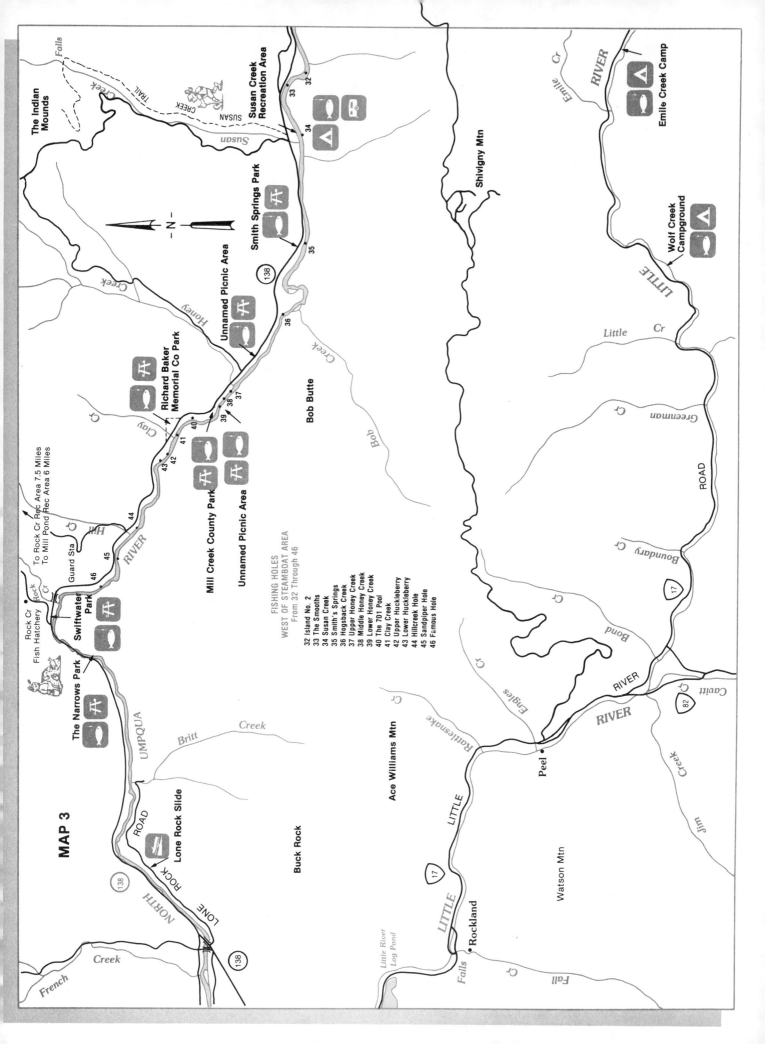

MAP 3

The Indian Mounds

Falls

French Creek

Rock Cr Fish Hatchery

To Rock Cr Rec Area 7.5 Miles
To Mill Pond Rec Area 6 Miles

Guard Sta

Rock Cr

UMPQUA RIVER

The Narrows Park

Swiftwater Park

NORTH

138

LONE ROCK ROAD

Lone Rock Slide

Britt Creek

Buck Rock

Clay Cr

Richard Baker Memorial Co Park

Honey Creek

Unnamed Picnic Area

Mill Creek County Park

Unnamed Picnic Area

40
41
42
43
44
45
46

39
38
37

36

Bob Butte

Bob Creek

– N –

138

Susan Creek

Susan Creek Recreation Area

Smith Springs Park

35

34

33

32

SUSAN CREEK TRAIL

Emile Cr

Emile Creek Camp

RIVER

Shivigny Mtn

LITTLE

Little Cr

Wolf Creek Campground

Greenman Cr

Boundary Cr

ROAD

17

Bond Cr

RIVER

Caitit Cr

82

Jim Creek

Peel

Eagles Cr

Rattlesnake Cr

Ace Williams Mtn

LITTLE LITTLE RIVER

17

Rockland

Little River Log Pond

Falls

Fall Cr

Watson Mtn

**FISHING HOLES
WEST OF STEAMBOAT AREA
From 32 Through 46**

32 Island No. 2
33 The Smooths
34 Susan Creek
35 Smith's Springs
36 Hogsback Creek
37 Upper Honey Creek
38 Middle Honey Creek
39 Lower Honey Creek
40 The 701 Pool
41 Clay Creek
42 Upper Huckleberry
43 Lower Huckleberry
44 Hillcreek Hole
45 Sandpiper Hole
46 Famous Hole

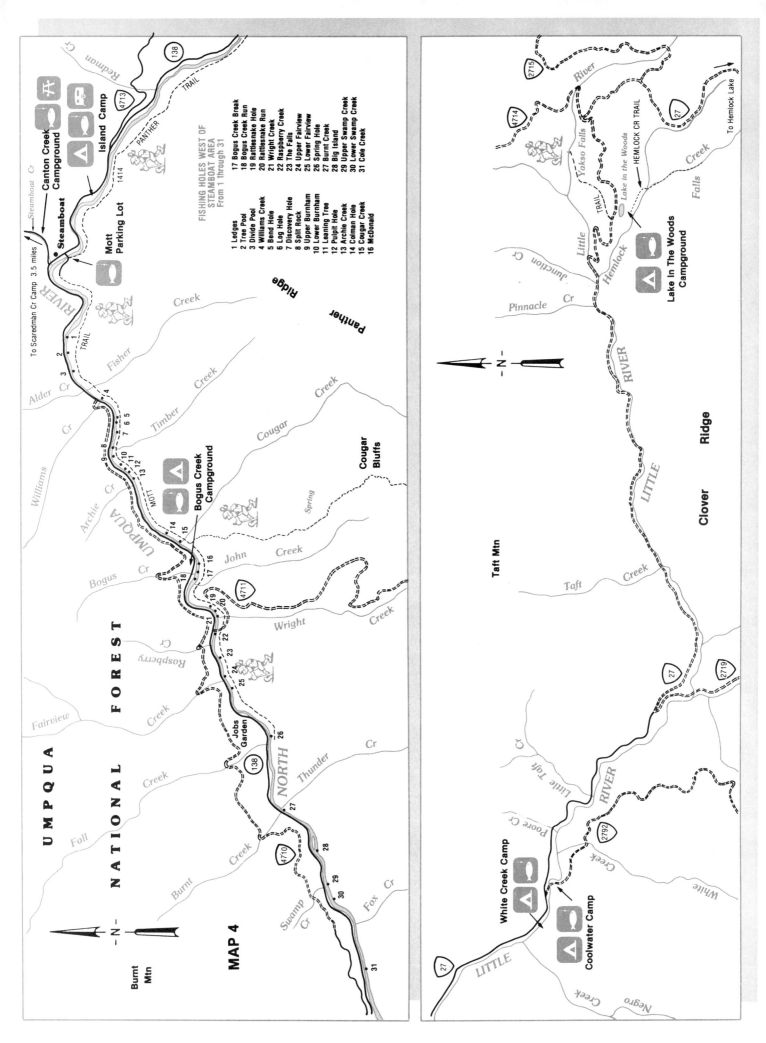

UMPQUA

NATIONAL   FOREST

MAP 4

-N-

Burnt Mtn

To Scaredman Cr Camp 3.5 miles

Canton Creek Campground

Island Camp

Steamboat

Mott Parking Lot

Redman Cr

138

4713

PANTHER   TRAIL

1414

FISHING HOLES WEST OF
STEAMBOAT AREA
From 1 through 31

1 Ledges
2 Tree Pool
3 Divide Pool
4 Williams Creek
5 Bend Hole
6 Log Hole
7 Discovery Hole
8 Split Rock
9 Upper Burnham
10 Lower Burnham
11 Leaning Tree
12 Pulpit Hole
13 Archie Creek
14 Colman Hole
15 Cougar Creek
16 McDonald

17 Bogus Creek Break
18 Bogus Creek Run
19 Rattlesnake Hole
20 Rattlesnake Run
21 Wright Creek
22 Raspberry Creek
23 The Falls
24 Upper Fairview
25 Lower Fairview
26 Spring Hole
27 Burnt Creek
28 Big Island
29 Upper Swamp Creek
30 Lower Swamp Creek
31 Cole Creek

STEAMBOAT   RIVER

Fisher   Creek

Panther   Ridge

Alder Cr

Williams   Cr

Timber   Creek

Cougar   Creek

Archie   Cr

UMPQUA   MOTT

Bogus Creek Campground

Bogus   Cr

John   Creek   Cr

4711

Wright   Creek

Raspberry   Cr

Cougar Bluffs

Spring   Creek

Fairview   Creek

Jobs Garden

138

NORTH   Thunder   Cr

27

4710

Burnt   Creek

Fall   Creek

Swamp   Cr

Fox   Cr

Lake In The Woods Campground

Yakso Falls

TRAIL

Little   Hemlock

Junction   Cr

Pinnacle   Cr

HEMLOCK CR TRAIL

Lake in the Woods

2715   River

4714

27

To Hemlock Lake

Creek   Falls

-N-

Taft Mtn

LITTLE   RIVER

Clover   Ridge

Taft   Creek

Little Taft   Cr

27

2719

White Creek Camp

Coolwater Camp

LITTLE   RIVER

Poore Cr

2792

White   Creek

Negro   Creek

27

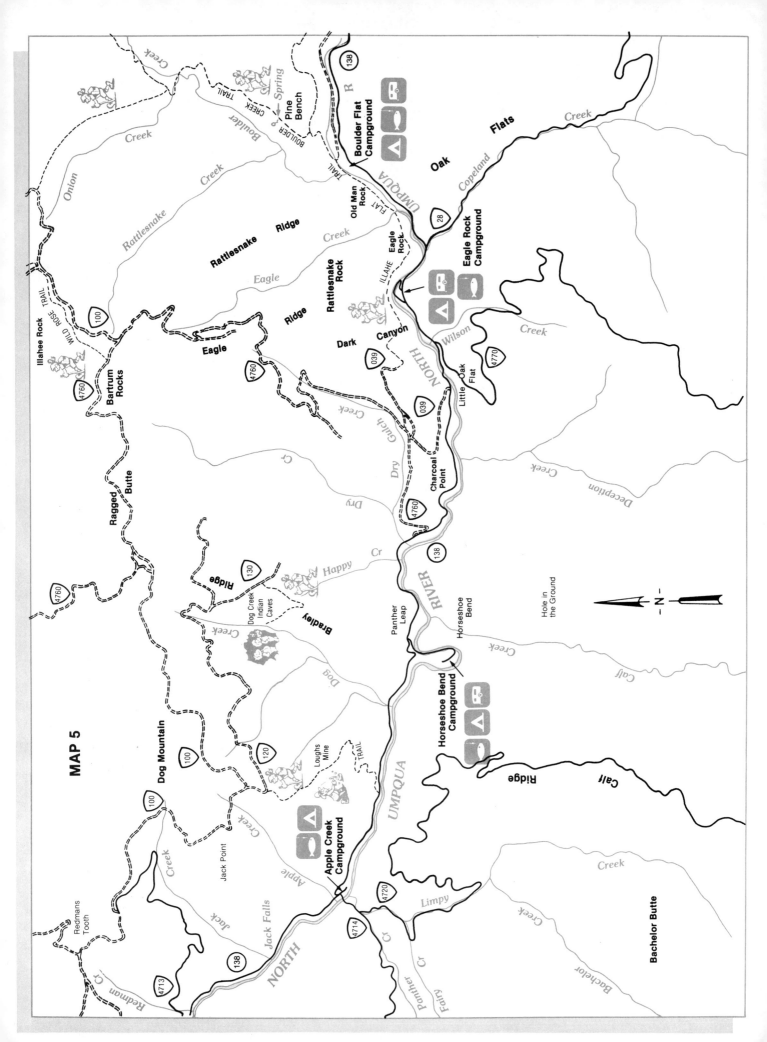

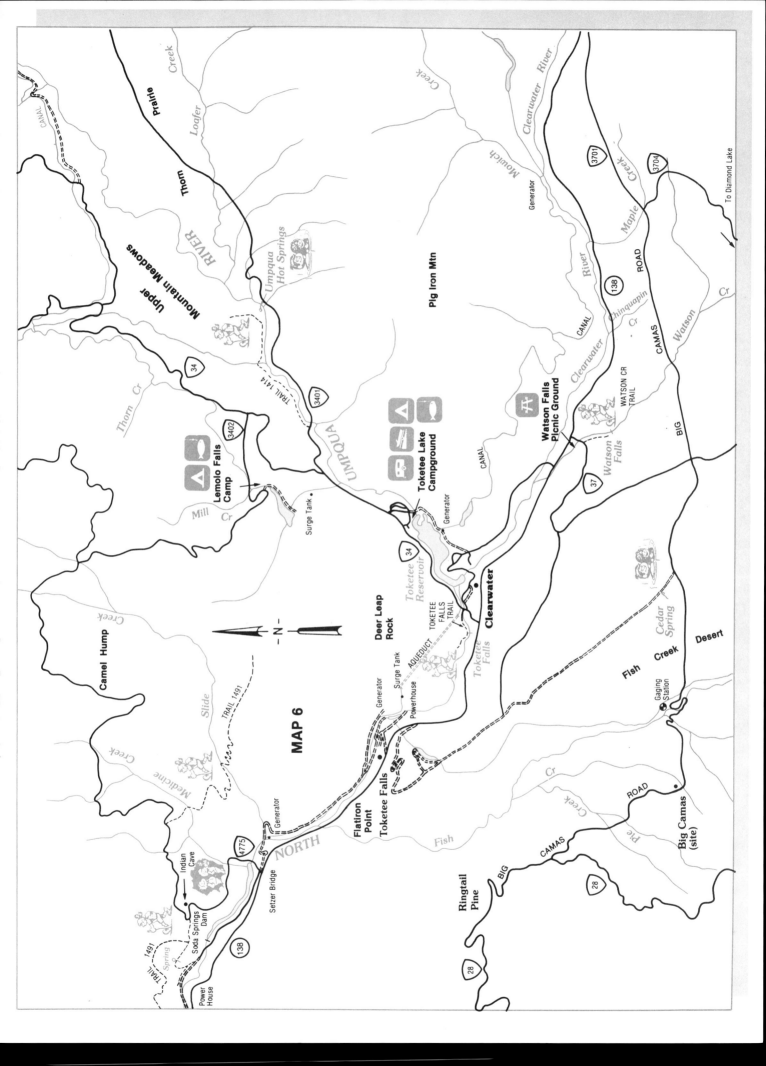

MAP 6

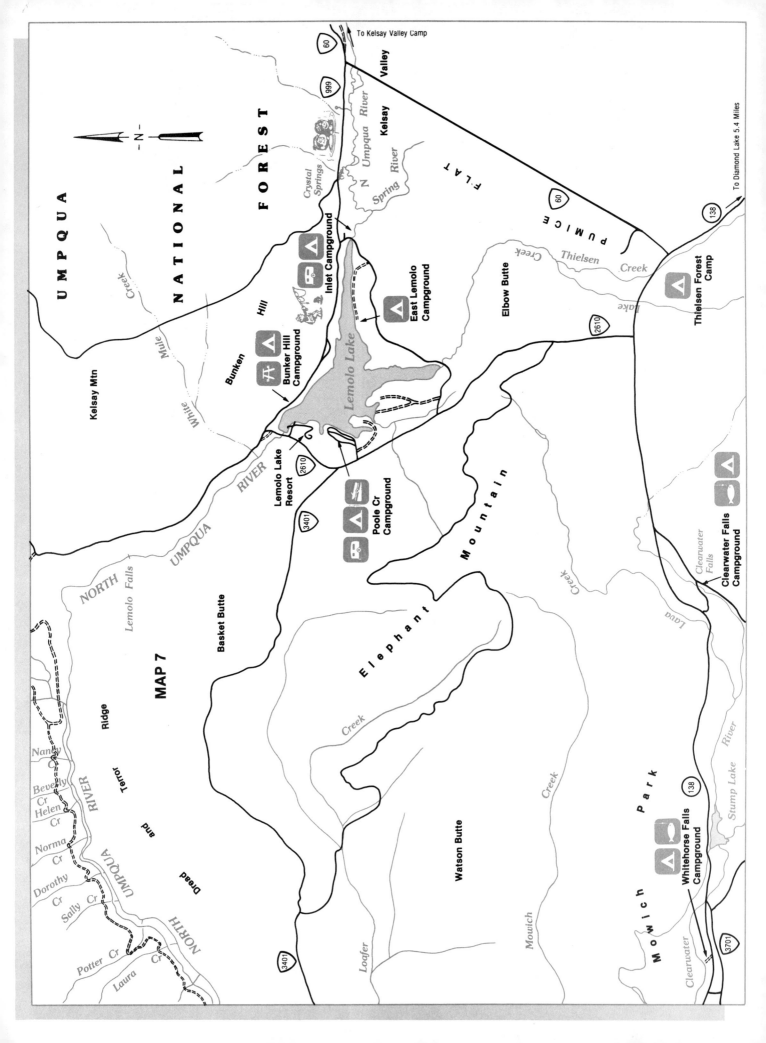

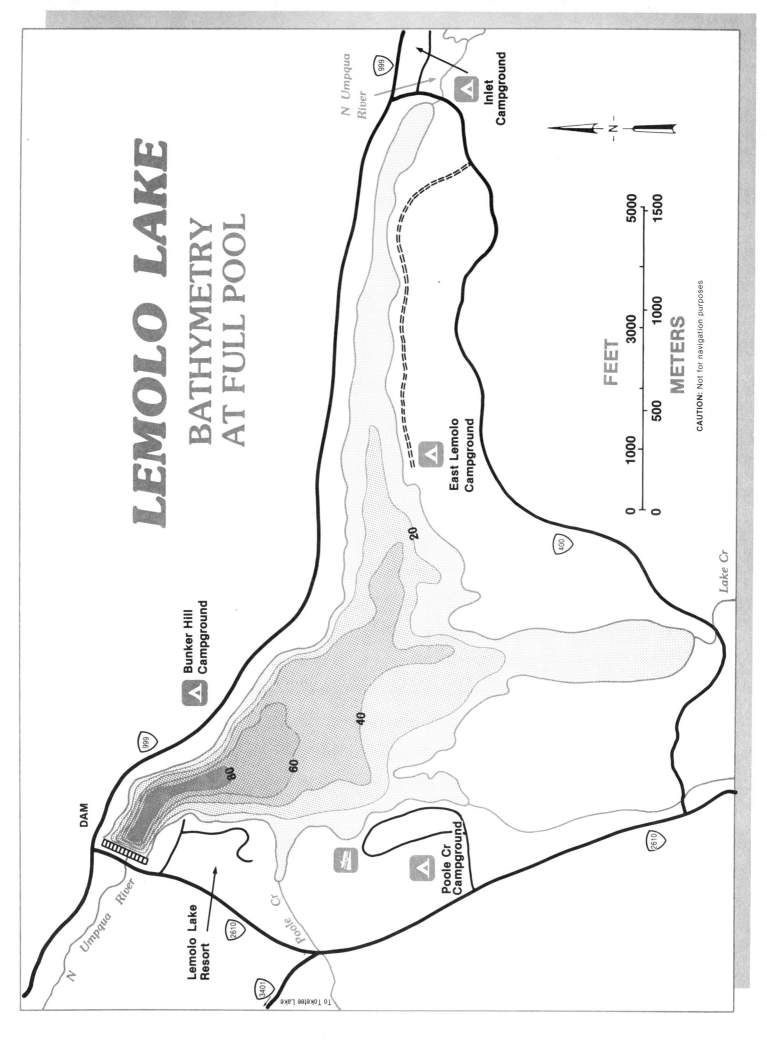

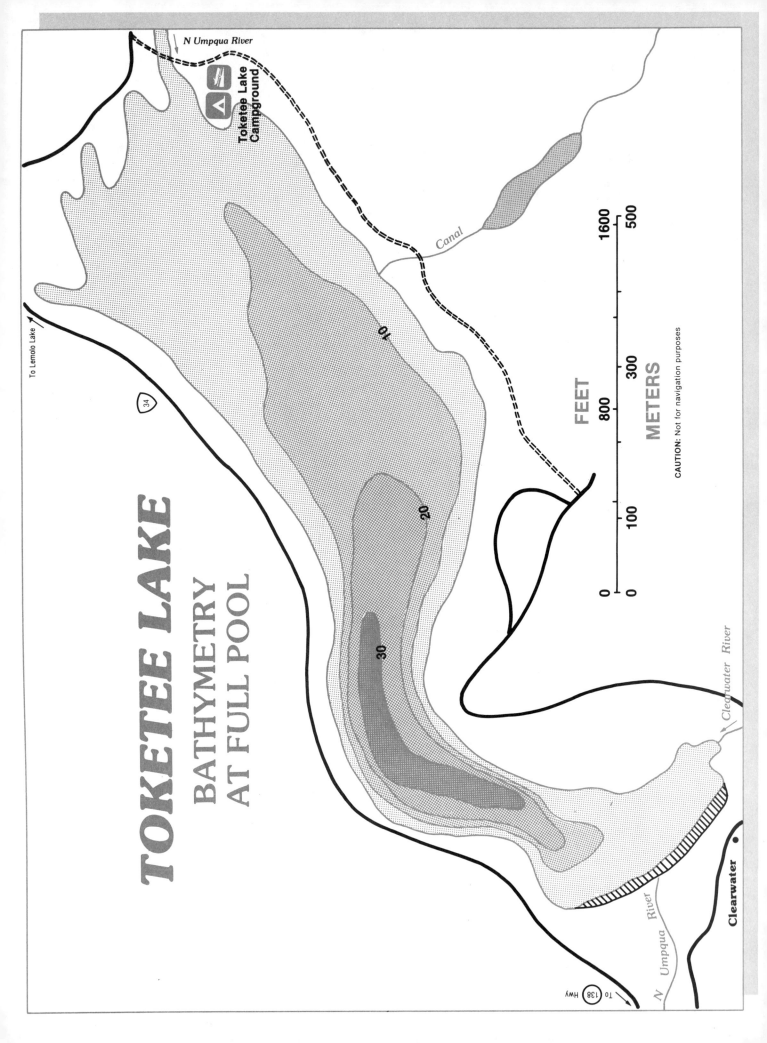

TOKETEE LAKE

BATHYMETRY AT FULL POOL

N Umpqua River

Toketee Lake Campground

To Lemolo Lake

34

Canal

10

20

30

To Lemolo Lake

FEET

0   800   1600

METERS

0   100   300   500

CAUTION: Not for navigation purposes

N Umpqua River

Clearwater River

To 138 Hwy

Clearwater

Chapter 5

LAKES of the NORTH UMPQUA

LINDA, CHARLINE, & CALAMUT LAKES

Location: From Lemolo Lake, travel east on Forest Road 999 to its junction (a fork in the road) with Forest Road 60; take Road 60 (the left fork) for approximately 2.5 miles to its junction with Spur Road 700; turn northwest on Spur Road 700, travel approximately 2.5 miles, and turn north on Spur Road 740. Spur Road 740 deadends at Lake Linda and the Calamut Lake Trailhead (Trail 1494).

All three lakes are stocked with brook trout annually by the Oregon Department of Fish and Wildlife. Most trout you catch will be from 6 to 8 inches long; however, there are a few holdovers — fish who survive more than the one summer — that grow as large as 14 inches long. The fishing provides an excuse to go there, but the big attraction of the area is its pristine beauty and solitude. The author and his wife hiked in to Calamut Lake during Labor Day weekend 1987; no other people were encountered. The entire area gets very little use.

The trail to Calamut Lake is an easy 1.5-mile hike. Calamut Lake has a few stretches of white sandy beach that provide a place to swim without roiling the water with the mud that usually covers the floor of alpine lakes (a swim is a welcome refreshment after the pummy dust bath provided by the roads to Lake Linda, and the ankle-deep dust on the hiking trail).

There is one primitive campsite with a picnic table and pit toilet at the trailhead, and another at Calamut Lake.

MAIDU LAKE AND LAKE LUCILE

Maidu Lake is the source of the North Umpqua River, and can be reached by the North Umpqua Trail (No. 1414) from Kelsay Camp on the North Umpqua side, or from Miller Lake on the Winema Forest side; the trail is about 8 miles long if you come in from Kelsay Camp, and about 3.5 miles if you come in from Miller Lake. Maidu and Lucile are both stocked with brook trout. The trail parallels the North Umpqua below

Maidu, and brook trout can also be taken from this upper stretch of the river.

Horse packers use Kelsay Camp as a jumping-off spot for trips into the high Cascades and along the Pacific Crest Trail, so this segment of trail 1414 is maintained wide and smooth to accommodate horses and mules. Since most of the surrounding country is alpine meadow, the mosquitos, black flies, and no-see-ums are particularly fierce. There is no way to avoid them, but you can lessen your discomfort by limiting your travels in the area to late August and September.

Since both are shallow lakes, they can be fairly productive for fly angling. The Mosquito is a good fly pattern for surface fishing, and small dark patterns like a Peacock & Alder produce well for bottom fishing.

Spin fishermen will do well with small coppery wobbling spoons and small spinners with dark bodies and brass or copper blades. Bait fishermen can do well fishing Pine Borer larvae gathered from under the loose bark of windfall trees, or single red salmon eggs, or worms.

LEMOLO RESERVOIR

Lemolo Reservoir covers an area of about 420 acres; it is the largest reservoir on the North Umpqua River and yields the best lake fishing and the largest resident fish in the system. Trout a foot long are the norm, and trout weighing several pounds are commonplace.

To reach Lemolo: Turn north off Highway 138 at Lemolo Junction (Forest Road 2610).

CAMPGROUNDS:

There are four campgrounds on Lemolo: Inlet, East Lemolo, Poole Creek, and Bunker Hill. See Chapter 11 for further details.

Lemolo can be successfully fished from the shore, but you'll have a better chance of catching the trophy trout this lake is famous for if you fish from a boat. If you don't own a boat, rentals are available at the resort.

Most of the trophy-sized fish caught in Lemolo are

taken by anglers trolling from boats equipped with electronic fish locators, who fish a deep diving 9-inch-long Rebel or Rapala lure, colored silver and blue (which resembles a small rainbow trout) or gold belly, black back (which resembles the roach, or suckers, that infest the lake), and troll back and forth across the deep hole just upstream of the dam. The larger fish are usually near the bottom and can be caught without using an electronic spotter, but the job is more tedious and time consuming. Begin trolling at a depth of about 40 feet, and adjust the depth of troll downward several feet after each 3 or 4 passes over the hole; when you get a strike, keep the troll at that depth. Troll the lure just fast enough to make the wiggling action work.

If the fish are feeding on or near the bottom, they can be fished for with metallic blue or green Stee-Lees or similar fluttering spoons. Beginning 200 yards upstream of the dam, let your boat drift down over the deep hole; lower the lure over the side of the boat and let it sink to the bottom, close the bail on your reel, and jig the lure up and down (pick the rod tip up as high as you can reach, then allow the lure to flutter back down on a slack line until you feel it touch bottom, then repeat the process). Stay away from the dam! The flow of water over Lemolo dam is regulated by automatic machinery, which starts and stops without warning; get too close to the dam, and you put yourself at risk of being sucked into the machinery.

Traditional trolling techniques — flashers trailing a baited hook — are most effective if you troll near the shoreline; particularly in places like the steep drop-offs along the north shore from Bunker Hill to Inlet, or along the Pumice cliff on the eastern side of the Thielsen Creek arm. Troll no more than 40 feet from shore, and just fast enough to make the flashers work. Flasher trolling will take rainbow and brook trout, but does not take many large brown trout.

Favorite spots for fishing from shore are generally the places which allow access to deeper water — that is, along the north shore around Bunker Hill, and along the south shore in the area between the Thielsen Creek and Poole Creek arms.

Fly fishing Lemolo can be rewarding, though one seldom catches fish larger than 16 inches on a fly. The best times for fly fishing are before noon and late evening. Early in the day, as the sun warms the surface of the lake, the fish will feed in shallower water, like the area along the south shore of the lake near Poole Creek campground. Fish a bright pattern, such as a Poodle Dog or a Carson Coachman, on a long, light leader (2- or 3-pound test) with a floating line. If the fish are not feeding on the surface, fish a dark pattern, like a Grenade Fly or Peacock & Alder, on a short, 3-pound test leader and a sinking line. (Lemolo fish, especially the larger ones, seem to be extremely leader shy, and heavier leaders simply won't catch fish).

In areas 25 to 30 feet deep, large trout can be taken with a fly rod and sinking fly line as follows: cast as far as you can, then strip off another thirty feet of line as the fly line begins sinking (so it will sink straight down); wait until the line has settled on the bottom, then retrieve it in twitches as slowly as a bug crawls.

When wet fly fishing the surface, let all ripples made by the line falling on the water subside, then retrieve the fly in short, quick jerks.

Trolling a fly can also be productive, and will usually produce the largest fly-caught trout on Lemolo. Use a floating line and a 9- to 12-foot leader tapering to 2-pound test. Tie a large, bright pattern, like a No. 6 Dark Spruce Fly or a No. 6 or No. 8 Poodle Dog on the tip, and a small buggy-looking fly, like a No. 14 Mosquito Larva or a No. 12 Light Cahill, on a dropper 12 inches to 18 inches up from the tip. This rig (according to some fishermen) imitates a minnow chasing a bug; whether or not the fish sees it as such, it is effective. Most of the fish caught will strike the dropper fly.

Lemolo occasionally provides good late evening dry fly action, especially when enough breeze is blowing to riffle the surface of the water. Let your boat drift free, and cast your fly across and upwind, to get as long a drag-free float as possible. Since the fish will be cruising, and their movements are random, trying to cast to a particular fish is futile; cast the fly out and let it drift, and the fish will find it.

A No. 16 Mosquito (or a No. 16 Adams, if you don't have a Mosquito in your fly box), tied on the lightest leader you have, will usually be the most productive dry fly. Other flies that occasionally produce fish include a Grasshopper (fished downwind from high bluff banks, like the one between The Thielsen and Poole Creek arms), a size 12 or 14 Light Cahill, and a small Black Gnat.

Later in the season, when the summer sun has warmed up the water in the lake, many of the fish will move up toward the inlet, because the water flowing into the lake is cooler and carries more oxygen and food than the still waters of the lake. These fish can be taken by bottom-fishing large, dark flies that resemble stonefly nymphs, or by fishing Light Cahill wets or leech imitations. Use either a sinking line, or weighted flies and a long leader on a floating line.

TOKETEE LAKE

Toketee is a relatively small (80 acres) reservoir located about 12 miles downstream of Lemolo, at the confluence of the North Umpqua and Clearwater Rivers.

Salmon fishing, Douglas County, circa 1910. Douglas County Museum photo

To Reach Toketee: turn off Highway 138 onto Forest Road 34 at Toketee Junction. Toketee Lake Campground is located adjacent to F.R. 34 at the inlet. See the chapter on campgrounds for further information.

Toketee produces good fish, but they are neither as large nor as plentiful as in Lemolo. It is shallower, and (possibly because it is fed by the Clearwater River) the water is clearer and cooler than Lemolo — so when the weather is hot and the fishing is lousy at Lemolo, you can sometimes improve your luck by moving to Toketee.

With few exceptions, the fishing methods described for Lemolo Lake work on Toketee. The productive trolling areas are along the south shore where the penstock dumps into the lake, and along the deep trench where the lake narrows down a few hundred yards upstream from the dam. Trolling the large plugs occasionally used

at Lemolo will probably be a waste of time at Toketee.

There are graveled parking areas along the north shore of the lake, and, because of the easy access, these are the areas usually fished by bank fishermen.

Fly fishermen usually pick the time when the fish are feeding near the surface, and concentrate their efforts in the shallow flats around the North Umpqua inlet at the upper end of the lake, and the Clearwater inlet at the lower end of the lake.

The North Umpqua between Toketee Dam and the canyon above Toketee Falls is excellent fly water, but must be fished cautiously; about halfway between the dam and the falls the river drops into a bedrock canyon with sheer walls. Confine yourself to the water upstream of the canyon. *Do not try to fish the canyon! It has no safe exit!*

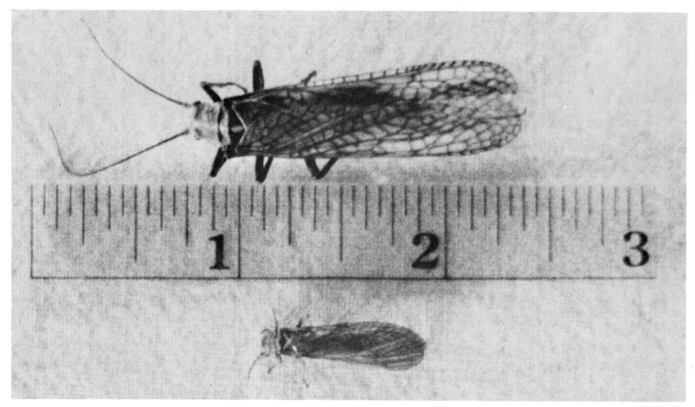

The salmon fly's color is a warm burnt orange (somewhat lighter in shade than ground paprika), with bright, olive-tinged yellow vermicular markings on the underside of its abdomen and thorax, and a yellow collar; its wings are diaphanous with olive brown veins. The smaller yellow stone is lemon yellow with iridescent vermiculations and an olive brown or orange collar; its wings are diaphanous with yellowish-brown veins. Top: Orange stonefly, also called salmon fly. Bottom: Golden Stone.

FOREBAYS

Forebays are small collecting reservoirs that gather extra water to run through the larger reservoirs for electric power production. There are several forebays around Lemolo and Toketee; all of them can be fished about the same way you fish the larger reservoirs — except that most aren't worth the trouble it takes to fish them by boat. Forebays are generally at the bitter end of a bad road, and because they are smaller and shallower, they are warmer, and the few fish they hold are usually harder to catch than the fish in the reservoirs. The forebays come into their own when the larger reservoirs are crowded with people. At such times, you can hunt one out and usually have it to yourself to season your fishing with solitude.

Clearwater No. 1 Reservoir, located approximately 2.5 miles north of Highway 138 (turn on Forest Road 4780 at Stump Lake, then turn west on spur road 300), is stocked with brook and rainbow trout. Fish Creek Reservoir (turn south from Highway 138 on Forest Road 37 at Watson Falls, then turn west on Road 3701, and south again on spur road 300) is stocked with brook and rainbow trout. Lemolo No. 1 Forebay is located approxi-

mately 6 miles downstream of Lemolo Dam, and is stocked with brook, brown, and rainbow trout; get there by following the Forest Road on the north shore of the river below Lemolo Dam. Lemolo No. 2 Forebay is on the mountain top overlooking Toketee Reservoir; it is stocked with brown, brook, and rainbow trout, and is sited with a Forest Service campground (see Chapter 11 for further information).

SODA SPRINGS RESERVOIR

Soda Springs reservoir was formed by damming a stretch of the North Umpqua that is hemmed in by sheer rock walls; the reservoir covers about 30 acres, and is a little more than 30 feet deep at its deepest point.

To reach Soda Springs: Turn off Highway 138 onto Forest Road 4774, Medicine Creek Road, then immediately turn left on spur road 012; road 012 parallels the south shore of the reservoir. Soda Springs Trail branches off road 012 about halfway down the lake; road 012 dead ends a mile or so below Soda Springs Dam at the Boulder Creek Trailhead.

Access is severely limited, but the fishing is good.

Fishing Soda Springs from the shore is extremely difficult, because of the steep cliff walls around the lake, but there is a spot at the lower end of the reservoir where a small rubber boat or car-topper can be launched. The reservoir can be fished much more effectively from a boat.

Neither trolling nor fly fishing are particularly productive on Soda Springs. The most productive fishing method is to row to the upper end of the reservoir and allow the boat to drift down toward the dam, and either cast and retrieve small spinners, or cast out a worm behind a split shot and let it sink to the bottom and drag along behind the boat as it drifts.

The fly fishing possibilities at Soda Springs are limited to trolling flies, as described under Lemolo Lake (above), casting grasshoppers to cruising fish at the upper end of the lake, and fishing stonefly nymph imitations on the bottom at the inlet.

Stay away from the dam! As with other reservoirs on the North Umpqua, the machinery that regulates the flow of water through the dam is automated, and may start without warning at any time.

WINCHESTER RESERVOIR

There is only one public boat access to Winchester — just east of the 1-mile post on Page Road; the landing is unimproved and ridiculously steep, adequate for launching a drift boat or rowboat, but not a motorboat. That's just as well — every homeowner along the lakeshore has a private boat landing and a motorboat, so there are already too many ski boats and speedboats on the lake to make it worth an angler's time.

However, the water where the river tails out into the upper end of the lake is worth an evening's fishing. The waters along both sides of the island at the upper end of the reservoir are excellent trout water, if fished either with a light fly rod or ultralight spinning gear. If you fly fish it, a No. 10 Mormon Girl or No. 14 Light Cahill nymph are effective wet patterns, and Light Cahill dry flies, sizes No. 16 and No. 10, fairly imitate the bugs that hatch off in the late evening.

On spinning gear, the wet flies named above — fished on a leader behind a split shot — will, at most times, be more effective than spinning lures. If you have no flies, small silver, white, or red lures will take fish.

When salmon and steelhead are moving through, the hole at the head of the lake is a good spot for "plunking" — anchoring your boat in midstream at the top of the hole and still-fishing a cluster of eggs on bottom, or dangling a Hot Shot or Wee Wart over the side on a long line for a mid-water lure.

OTHER LAKES OF THE NORTH UMPQUA

The locations of the lakes and ponds below are described by Township and Range; the location and even the numbering systems for minor roads may change from time to time, but a Township and Range location description assures that you will be able to locate the named lakes on a fireman's map, and find your way to them if a developed route exists.

These are not by any means the only lakes that hold fish: there are dozens, perhaps hundreds, of beaver ponds and logjam holdbacks along the North Umpqua corridor. Some are listed in *Lakes of the Fremont, Rogue, Siskiyou, Siuslaw, Umpqua & Winema National Forests* — a joint publication of the Oregon Department of Fish & Wildlife and the U.S. Forest Service. Others can only be found by stomping around and stumbling on them by accident — which is one of the things that makes exploring an exciting pastime: you sometimes manage to stumble on something new, something you didn't know existed. Most of the lakes that don't dry up in the summer hold fish; most of the smaller ones are isolated enough and see little enough human use that hiking in to find them can be a rewarding experience even if you don't catch any fish.

Bull Pup and Fuller Lakes are alpine lakes in Township 25 South, Range 3 East. Bull Pup is a shallow lake of about 2 acres' size in section 6. Fuller, in section 18, covers approximately 3 acres. Both are stocked with brook trout. There are other lakes in this township — Bradley Lake, Loletta Lakes, and a few beaver ponds — but they may or may not hold fish.

Lake-in-the-Woods, Limpy Lake, Cinderella Pond, and Hemlock Meadows Reservoir are located in the Little River Drainage in Township 27 South, Range 1 East. Hemlock (section 27) covers about 20 acres and is 30 feet deep; Lake-in-the-Woods (section 17) covers 4 acres; the other two are small ponds. All four hold rainbow trout, and Hemlock is stocked with kokanee. There is an improved campground with flush toilets at Lake-in-the-Woods, and a boat launching ramp and primitive camp at Hemlock.

Big Twin, Lake, Little Twin Lake, and Buckhead Camp Pond are located in Township 27 South, Range 2 East. The Twin Lakes (section 9) are stocked with brook trout, and Buckhead Pond (section 31) is stocked with rainbow trout. There are primitive campgrounds at Buckhead Pond, and just north of Big Twin Lake. Big and Little Twin are deep alpine tarns, 14 and 10 acres respectively; Buckhead Pond coves less than an acre.

Skookum Lake, located in Township 28 South, Range 4 East, section 33, is another alpine tarn; it covers about 15 acres and is stocked with brook trout.

Chapter 6 ———————————————————

FISHING the NORTH UMPQUA RIVER and its TRIBUTARIES

THE UPPER RIVER – MAIDU TO TOKETEE

Upstream of Lemolo, most of the fish caught will be small brook trout, except in the autumn, when rainbow trout move up into the river. Fishing in this stretch of river is extremely difficult; the water is as clear as gin, coursing over a white pumice sand bottom, too swift to wade safely, cold, and full of logjams and grassy hummocks. To keep the fish from spooking on sight, they must be approached cautiously. When you do hook into large fish, you seldom land them – 2-pound test and lighter leaders are required equipment if you want to hook fish, and a 10- or 11-inch fish will run for a logjam and tangle up and break off almost every time.

The only baits the author has found effective in the upper river are white mealworms, pine borer larvae (another white worm), and red single salmon eggs.

The more effective fly patterns are imitations of the mosquitoes, black flies, and no-see-ums that make the angler's life a misery – No. 16 Mosquito Larva, No. 14 Peacock & Alder, and No. 14 or No. 16 Light Cahill nymph. When imitations of natural pests don't work, the best bet becomes a very bright fly – a Carson Coachman or Mormon Girl in size No. 8 or No. 10.

A fly angler who knows the value of a split-shot on the leader, about 18 to 24 inches up from the fly, will catch more fish. The brook trout hang in eddies or relatively slow-moving water, generally along inside bends of the river. Rainbow trout hang in slightly faster water, in places where the current has undercut banks, in the rip between fast current and eddies, and under or just downstream of logjams. In each case, the split shot is needed to get the fly down to the fish; rather than casting to the fish, strip the leader out through the tip of the rod, and dabble the fly in likely looking places the way you would fish with a cane pole and line.

Between Lemolo and Toketee, the river is still swift, but its character has changed a little: there are fewer logjams and no grass hummocks in the river, and the bottom is either gravelled or bedrock. The same patterns suggested above still work, except that a large orange stonefly imitation, such as a Kolzer Dark Caddis, should be added to the fly selection.

THE CLEARWATER RIVER

The Clearwater is a small river that can be extremely frustrating to fish. It holds some nice-sized brook and (occasionally) rainbow trout, but the water is as clear as the mountain air you breathe while fishing. In such clear water, the fish will see you and spook long before you're in casting range, and you must suit your fishing methods to the conditions:

• Use 2-pound test or lighter leaders.

• Particularly on the upper reaches of the river, whether or not you catch a fish is more dependent on how stealthily you approach the river than on what type of lure you use.

• Only rarely will you see trout rising to take surface flies; the most productive way to fly fish the Clearwater is downstream wet fly fishing.

• Spinning lures don't seem to work very well; the splash and glitter spooks the fish.

The common hatches on the Clearwater are an orange stonefly over an inch long, a brown caddis about half an inch long, and a blue mayfly with mottled brown wings that can be imitated with a No. 10 or No. 12 Adams. When conditions are right – that is, when the bugs are on the water – a No. 18 Mosquito and a Grasshopper may also be used.

In its upper reaches (above Stump Lake), the Clearwater is an oddity: it has a white sand bottom, more aquatic vegetation than you might expect at that altitude, and most of the fish's cover is provided by undercut banks and deadfall trees. The water is as clear as air; wading it is easy, but deceptive: because it is so clear, a hole that looks a foot deep may be 4 or 5 feet deep.

Whether or not you fish the upper end of the Clearwater depends on your tolerance for frustration. The fish will usually see you long before you see it, and will spook from every shadow you cast and every move you make.

The upper river is accessible from Highway 138 and Clearwater Falls Campground, but the farther away from the easily accessible areas you get, the better the fishing will be. The area near Clearwater Falls gets fished heavily in the summer, and the area a mile downstream (that you must travel cross-country to reach) hardly gets fished at all.

Stump Lake is a reservoir on the Clearwater River, adjacent to the south side of Highway 138 on Forest Road 641, at an elevation of 3871 feet. It covers an area of about 11 acres and is shallow — about 10 feet deep at its deepest point. Its name is descriptive: the lake bottom is covered with tree stumps, and a forest of stumps jut above water level over the upstream half of the lake.

Where Road 641 meets the lake, a rowboat or a canoe can be slid into the lake; however, the lake is too shallow and too overgrown with underwater vegetation to allow safe use of a motor.

The bottom of Stump Lake is covered with aquatic vegetation, so when baitfishing, you should use a floating bait rig (see the chapter on terminal tackle) so the bait floats clear of the bottom. If fly fishing, do your fishing during the times when a breeze riffles the surface of the lake, so the fly line landing on the water doesn't spook the fish.

The water in the lower Clearwater River is still as gin-clear as in the upper river, but is easier to fish because of the terrain. Instead of relatively smooth water flowing over white sand, the lower Clearwater consists mostly of broken water pouring from pothole to pothole in volcanic rock. The airbubbles and turbulence provide better cover for the fish and fishermen: the fish hold in the bottoms of the potholes, and, since most of the fish are brook trout, about all that's needed for success is to get a lure down to the fish.

THE FLY FISHING ONLY AREA

A couple of factors work together to make fishing the "fly fishing only" area easier for you. First, natural selection has made the fish a pretty good instinctive mathematician: it won't move to take a bug if, to do so, it has to expend more energy than the bug will provide when eaten — so if there are several bugs showing, the fish is likely to be taking either the largest or the most numerous. Secondly, rainbows are finned opossums: they will eat anything that doesn't eat them first. Not being critics, they will humbly and gratefully inhale the fly you offer, without giving much thought to its genus or species or your technique. Brown trout on the upper river, below Soda Springs, will occasionally become selective, but even then can usually be tempted to strike a fly that resembles a minnow (Poodle Dog, Carson Coachman, or Bucktail Coachman).

Even during heavy hatches, wet flies will usually catch the largest and the most fish. Most of the better hatches on the upper river are either stoneflies or a large gray mayfly with brown-mottled wings. The trout will be taking mayflies that have been washed under by turbulence and are struggling to get airborne, or will be taking stoneflies buzzing and flopping along in the surface film, depositing eggs. Given those circumstances, a dragging fly, fished across and downstream, will more closely resemble the natural and catch more fish than a drag-free float. The only place you're likely to find fish feeding exclusively on dry flies — bugs sitting high and dry on top of the surface film — is in the long, slow, deep runs below Steamboat.

Sometimes the fishing is easy: the fish will be lined up 6 or 8 feet apart along the feeding slot, and each fish will be rising to its own rhythm. If the fish is rising every several seconds and leaving a swirl on the surface after it takes the bug, it will be taking larger bugs, one at a time, and can be caught by matching your presentation to its rise rhythm. If it is staying at or near the surface and sloshing around a lot, it is feeding by the mouthful on the smaller bugs that hatch out in swarms, and it will be more difficult to catch. When a fish is inhaling small bugs by the mouthful, you have two choices — either put a small fly near the fish and hope that (out of the swarm of bugs within its range of vision) it takes yours, or use the Ray Bergman principle (offer it something radically different). Both choices are frustrating — but when the fish is feeding on tiny dries on the lower river and rejecting everything you offer it, you may find easier fishing by moving a few miles upstream and fishing broken water.

A basic truism of fly fishing is that (with few exceptions) mass produced commercial flies are designed to catch fishermen, not fish. In defense of commercial tiers it should be noted that nobody ever made a good living just tying flies. A commercial tier makes so little per fly, and has to tie so many, that he is forced to avail himself of every shortcut available.

Still, look at the fly bins in any fly shop, and you'll see the sort of pink, mauve, chartreuse, gilt, and flash a New Orleans dandy would be ashamed to wear on his hat. Large, flashy flies do catch trout, but sparsely tied olive, brown, green, black, or yellow patterns consistently catch more trout.

All it takes to catch a steelhead is a snippet of red, white or chartreuse yarn tied on a bare hook (it catches fish, and costs virtually nothing). That being the case, why tie the 2/0 bug-eyed fluorescent monstrosities currently so popular with many anglers? A No. 4 fly of a more sedate standard pattern is easier to cast, makes a smaller splash when it hits the water, and will catch steelhead as well as a larger fly.

If you buy commercially-tied wet flies, rather than

Steamboat Area

Fishing Pools

1. Upper Island
2. Island
3. Surveyor
4. Bridge
5. Sawtooth
6. Hayden's Run
7. Sweetheart
8. Confluence
9. Station
10. Upper Boat
11. Lower Boat
12. Upper Kitchen
13. Kitchen
14. The Fighting Hole
15. Upper Mott
16. Middle Mott
17. Lower Mott
18. Glory
19. Gorden
20. Upper Maple Ridge
21. Maple Ridge
22. Jeannie
23. Abernathy
24. Upper Takahashi
25. Lower Takahashi
26. Knouse

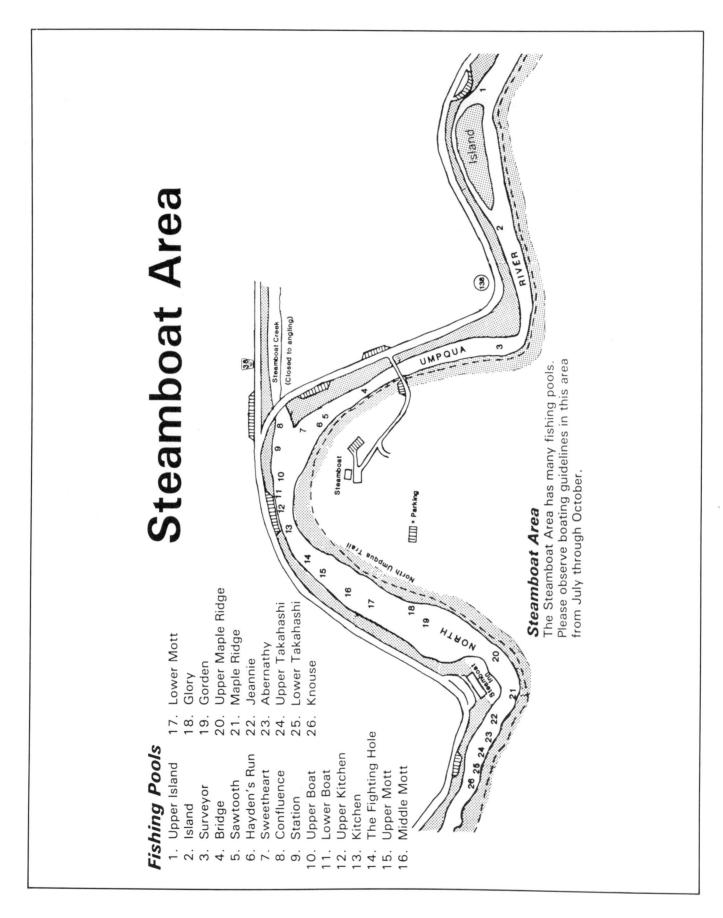

Steamboat Area

The Steamboat Area has many fishing pools. Please observe boating guidelines in this area from July through October.

tying your own, don't be afraid to give the fly a haircut before you fish with it. Commercial wet fly ties are likely to have too much tail, too much hackle, and too much wing. The tail should be visible up to a distance of about 3 feet underwater (only seldom will a fish move to take a fly that floats by more than 3 feet away). Two turns of hackle is usually sufficient, and more than two turns only serves to make the fly harder to sink. Bushy wings look good, but like bushy hackle, make the fly harder to sink.

Some patterns are supposed to tumble and bounce, and generally act like a panicked orphan; but most patterns are intended to swim upright through a drift, and won't catch fish unless they do. Make sure the fly swims properly before you fish it: tie it on your leader and dunk it in the current. If it does not swim upright, trim a few hairs off the wing on the low side and test it again. Keep removing hair from the low side until the fly swims straight and true.

The most commonly encountered steelhead flies on the North Umpqua are sizes No. 2 and No. 4; larger sizes are seldom used; size No. 6 flies are sometimes used during low water conditions or by anglers fishing lighter lines (No. 7 or No. 8). The rule of thumb is to use the smallest fly that will attract the fish's attention. That usually boils down to using larger, brighter colored patterns early in the season while the river is cold and green (before Independence Day), and changing to smaller sizes and darker colors once the water has cleared up and warmed.

Steelhead sometimes hang downstream of spawning salmon, picking up the spawn that floats out of the redd. When you fish water downstream of spawning redds, or when you fish early season off-color water, the Van Luven and similar patterns are effective. Other good choices for early season fishing or off-color water are bright, flashy patterns, like a Poodle Dog.

Once the water is clear enough you can see the bottom in deeper holes, darker patterns such as the Black Gordon, Silver Hilton, and Skunk are good producers.

By late August, the water is gin-clear and warm, the fish are scattered throughout the river and have become as spooky as wraiths from being fished over so much. To be successful, an angler must concentrate most of his energy on not scaring the fish. Lighter lines and smaller flies are the order of the day. Patterns with a lot of brown and yellow, smaller sizes of the dark patterns used during midseason, and nymph-like patterns such as the Grenade Fly and Peacock & Alder are good choices.

RIVER NOTES

The upper fishable limit of the fly fishing only section is the angling deadline about half a mile below Soda Springs Dam. The "no fishing" area and the deadline are both well-marked with signs posted on trees and power poles along the riverbank.

There are no "holes," as such, on the upper part of the fly fishing section; rather, the usual strategy is to "search" the water. Float a fly over any piece of water that looks slow enough to hold a trout, but don't waste any time: if you don't get a strike after a few casts, move on and fish somewhere else. When you do get a strike, there are likely to be more fish in the same area, unless the strike came in a pocket too small to hold more than a single fish.

The best access to this upper few miles of fly fishing water is by spur road 012 (Soda Springs Road) and Boulder Creek trail. This section of river gets very little angling pressure, but offers excellent rainbow and brown trout angling. The river is flowing down such a steep gradient that pocket water and eddies along the riverbank offer the best chance of hooking a fish. The Grasshopper, Grenade Fly, Peacock & Alder, Dark Spruce, and Mormon Girl all produce fish in this stretch of water.

From Boulder Creek campground to Oak Flat, the easiest access is from Highway 138. Use the same fly patterns listed above. The riffly, roily water around the boulders abreast of Eagle Rock campground is usually good for 2 or 3 trout.

At Oak Flat, Forest Road 4770 branches off to the south; for the next mile or so, the river can be accessed either from Highway 138 or by hiking down the riverbank from the picnic grounds on the south shore at Oak Flat. Oak Flat is also about where you can begin to expect to see a few light-colored caddis hatching. From Oak Flat downstream, keep the Peacock & Alder as a search pattern, but be on the lookout for fish taking the light caddis (which can be imitated with a Light Cahill) and yellow and orange stoneflies.

There is a parking area across from the Dry Creek store, and a trail down the hill to the river from the parking area. Some of the best trout fishing on the river can be had along this stretch, particularly in the hole straight down the hill from the store, the one below the rapids called Dog Wave, and the deep hole at Happy Rock.

From Charcoal Point to Panther Leap, there is little access to the river; only the hardiest souls clamber down over the cliff to the river, and those who do find precious little wadable water or casting room — but because that stretch of river gets so little fishing pressure, the trip is worth taking.

A few miles of river are accessible from the Horseshoe Bend Campground road, and by walking downstream from the campground. From about Panther Leap down, the gradient of the river begins to ease somewhat, and there are more wadable gravel bars and tailouts to fish. Orange Stonefly, Mormon Girl, and Peacock & Alder are good search patterns for this section of river.

From about Dog Creek on downstream to the campground at Apple Creek, the river settles into a pattern of long flat stretches broken up by short, steep rapids. This is also the part of the river where you will begin to see a few small yellow stoneflies (about 3/4 inches long) hatching out.

Apple Creek is also about the upper limit of the steelhead fishing. By August, steelhead will be scattered throughout the river, and you could possibly hook into one as far upriver as Eagle Rock — but since most of the fish go up the Steamboat Creek drainage, the largest concentration of fish will be found around and downstream of the mouth of Steamboat Creek.

Anglers who have been fishing the North Umpqua for several years know where the fish lay in the holes, and it isn't possible to describe precisely where to fish each hole — but neither is it entirely necessary. The best time of day for steelhead fishing is from daylight until the sun has been on the water about 2 hours; they can be caught any time of day, but in the early morning, they are relaxed, and haven't yet been spooked by fishermen.

Steelhead do most of their travelling between sunset and sunrise, and usually hold up in one spot during the day — and the first angler of the day who drifts a fly by a fish is the one most likely to catch it. Also, if you are on a hole at daylight, you can fish the "break" — the slick water tailout at the bottom end of the hole, where it breaks over into rapids — and have a fair chance of catching a fish that is still headed upstream and hasn't yet circled its wagons for the day.

From Apple Creek to Bogus Creek, a footpath (Trail 1414) parallels the south bank of the river; however, the trail offers only limited fishing access except in the area from the Surveyor Hole to Archie Creek (see map). Otherwise, the easiest access is from Highway 138: there are paved parking areas along the highway at most of the more popular holes.

Immediately west of milepost 39, a bridge crosses the North Umpqua; a fisherman's parking lot, the trailhead for the Mott segment of the North Umpqua Trail, and a large-scale map of the fishing holes on the section of the river near Steamboat are all at the south end of the bridge.

Polarized sunglasses are a most useful tool when you look for fish. In long stretches of swift, broken water, steelhead will hold up in pockets — eddies behind boulders — the way trout do; but in well defined holes, they will usually stop in the lower half of the hole. They may hang alongside a bedrock ledge, or under a bedrock undercut, or upstream, alongside, or downstream of a boulder. Only when they are moving are you likely to catch one on an open gravel bar with no cover near. Knowing this, you can pull off the highway and study a hole (wearing your sunglasses), and if a fish is in residence, you have a good chance of spotting it.

The hole at the confluence of Archie Creek is one of the more productive holes on the river; it is full of trout, regularly produces steelhead, and occasionally yields an accidental Chinook (keep in mind that any salmon caught upstream of Rock Creek should be released unharmed). The tailout of the hole is a good steelhead lie, especially early in the morning.

The deep, slow hole at the foot of Bogus Creek is also productive water, and the slick and riffly water just downstream also occasionally yields fish.

The Swamp Creek Hole, at the Umpqua National Forest boundary, is a good trout and steelhead hole.

The long, deep runs between Bogus Creek and Smith's Ford (the lower end of Susan Creek Park) provide good trout fishing. Late in the season, when dull days — with maybe a sprinkling of rain — are the norm, trout will feed on the surface most of the day; sometimes they are slurping bugs too small to be imitated by a fly, but usually they can be taken on a size 16 Light Cahill. The feeding fish will turn on and off with no seeming logic; they will rise for several minutes, then stop — sometimes for a few minutes, sometimes for the better part of an hour. If you are fishing a hole and the fish have been rising but have quit, take a coffee break: if you let the hole rest and wait awhile, the fish will begin rising again shortly.

The river between Susan Creek Park and the fly angling deadline at Rock Creek is limited of access, but offers excellent trout fishing throughout the year; this is the part of the river where you may expect to occasionally hook into a cutthroat. Most of the steelhead caught in this section of river are caught early in the run — during the month of June, are transients en route to the spawning grounds, and won't hold tight in the holes the way they do higher up in the river.

The 700 feet of river from the fly angling deadline to the marker above the mouth of Rock Creek is closed to all angling to protect the fish.

Although most anglers who fish the half-mile of river below the mouth of Rock Creek are after salmon or steelhead, the pocket water is full of native cutthroat trout: on an afternoon in October of 1986, in the middle of a downpour, the author caught and released almost a dozen cutthroat that averaged about 9 inches in length, in the space of about 20 minutes.

Chapter 7

DRIFT BOATING the NORTH UMPQUA

The upper end of the river, from Boulder Flat down, can be floated by rubber raft or kayak at higher water levels but is not navigable by hard boat. Angling from a floating device is not permitted upstream of Glide, but if you plan to make a recreational float of the upper river, maps and information on boating regulations and river conditions are available from the Forest Service (see appendix I).

From Glide to The Forks, the river is usually floatable in a hard boat the year around, and fishing from a boat is allowed.

BEFORE YOU LAUNCH YOUR BOAT

A successful drift down the river begins with a planning session at home. Good planning will help you avoid foreseeable misadventures and assure that you are prepared to cope with the unforeseen when it occurs.

Don't trust your memory — make a written checklist of things you need to do to and the gear you plan to take. Mark each task off the list as you complete it and mark each piece of gear off the list as it is loaded into your vehicle, then run through the gear checklist again at the boat landing as you load the gear into your boat.

Check your automobile and boat trailer. Check the fluid levels in your automobile, and the air level in all tires, including trailer and spare tires. Check the trailer: do the winch, loading roller, and taillights all work? Does the trailer hitch work properly, and are the safety chains in good shape? Are the boat tie-down hooks on the trailer in good condition?

Give your boat a safety check: is it in safe, usable condition? Is it properly tied down on the trailer, and are the tie-downs in good condition? Is the drain plug in? Have you loaded all your gear? Is the gear properly stowed, so it won't blow or bounce out en route to the river?

Make sure your "just in case" gear is loaded. Do you have a tow rope so you can be pulled out, or a shovel, so you can dig yourself out, if you get stuck on a muddy boat landing?

Scout the river. Realize that river conditions and rapids can change drastically with a slight fluctuation in water level. Watch the river stage reading in the local newspaper every day for several days before your trip; any single reading will be one day out of date, but a series will tell you what the river level has been and where it is headed. If possible, talk to someone who has, within the last few days, run the stretch of river you plan to run, so new obstructions or water conditions won't take you by surprise.

Safety

The most important piece of safety gear is your own common sense; always use it.

Before making a drift trip, evaluate your own physical condition. Don't saddle yourself with a longer drift or a heavier load than you can comfortably handle.

If you begin to tire before the end of a drift, either stop and rest or let someone else take the oars.

File a trip plan: that is, tell someone where you are going — where you plan to launch your boat, where and when you plan to take out, and leave instructions to begin a search if you have not either arrived home or telephoned by a stated time — and leave the same information written down, to insure against the vagaries of memory.

Distribute the load in the boat so the weight is centered. Cargo should be loaded with the heavier gear on bottom, to maintain as low a center of gravity as possible. The total load (cargo and passengers) should be centered so the boat rides level in the water fore-and-aft and right-to-left.

Hold a practice drill at the beginning of each trip, so everyone in the boat knows what is expected of them in an emergency:

• If you miscalculate, and find yourself about to crash into a rock (or any other obstruction), you should hit it bow first, not sideways. In a bow-on collision, you have a chance to spin off and regain control; in a side-on collision, your boat is likely to overturn.

• Tell your passengers to move to the high side of the

boat to keep it from overturning in a collision.

• If the boat is swamping or overturning, and you are forced to abandon ship, do so on the upstream side. Getting pinched between a boulder and a capsized boat can be fatal.

• Above all, don't panic — keep hold of the oars, keep rowing, and keep your wits. No situation is ever as bad as it will become after you panic. A drift boat will carry you safely through much worse situations than you think it will, and if you sink it, your lifejacket will save you.

That is, if you have a lifejacket and are wearing it. Lately, the bureaucrats have begun calling lifejackets PFDs — Personal Flotation Devices. However, the term lifejacket gives you a more exact idea of a PFD's true worth. The author owes his life, twice over, to lifejackets — and, having been adrift in a lifejacket in Class V rapids, knows that in such a situation, you'll be thinking about personal flotation in terms of staying alive.

The law requires you to carry a Coast Guard approved lifejacket for each person on board, and common sense suggests they be worn while running whitewater or drifting any unfamiliar stretch of river. Since you might well bump your head on a gunwale or a rock when you go overboard, the only lifejackets of any practical value on a whitewater river are those which have a collar that makes them hold your head out of the water and float you face-up; otherwise, you may become a floating drowning victim.

Each of your lifejackets should be tested at least once per season, and lifejackets that have lost their buoyancy should be replaced.

Err on the side of caution. Scout all rapids marked Class 3 or worse, and scout any water that puzzles you, or any place you hear rapids you can't see. "Scouting" means pulling your boat up onto the bank, walking down the bank to look at the rapids, and deciding on your course through the rapids before you return to your boat.

Unidentified man with fishing rod, boat and a number of fish on bank of Singleton Park, forks of the Umpqua River. Douglas County Museum photo

Learn to look for landmarks in a rapid when you scout it. Any rapid bad enough to beg scouting will look different from a boat than it did from shore, and if you haven't picked out landmarks to guide and show you where to make your cuts, you'll get lost before you get through.

Keep all ropes not actually in use stowed away, and **never – ever**, under any set of circumstances – put your foot or hand in a bight of line. If the boat overturns, and you are hung up in a tangle of rope, you will probably drown.

Tape a railroad flare to each lifejacket with duct tape and throw a few extra into the boat's cargo box. If you are thrown into the river, and your lifejacket saves you, the next danger you face (particularly during the winter months) is hypothermia – an excessive loss of body heat. You can't start a fire with matches if your hands are numb from hypothermia and your fingers don't work properly – but railroad flares are so large even fingers numb with cold can get them fired up, and they burn hot enough to start a fire in the rain with wet wood.

Don't expect more from your anchor than it was designed to do. Solid lead pyramids are the most efficient drift boat anchors, yielding the surest anchorage for the least weight. Even so, drift boaters have a habit of using heavier than necessary anchors. Typically, a 14-foot boat will carry a 20-pound anchor, and a 16-foot boat will carry a 30-pounder, when all that's necessary for safe anchorage is a 15-pounder for a 14-foot boat, and a 20-pounder for a 16-foot boat.

Heavy anchors are hard to handle and can get you into trouble by allowing you to anchor in water too swift to be safe. Lighter anchors are easier to handle and will not grab bottom in swift water.

Finally, rowing a boat is a sober person's job. Alcohol slows your reflexes and impairs your judgment – both of which reduce your ability to cope with whitewater and increase the likelihood of trouble. Further, alcohol in the bloodstream reduces your resistance to hypothermia.

Carry a good first aid kit in your boat at all times and know how to use it. Pay particular attention to techniques for treating hypothermia and reviving drowning victims. Find out before each trip whether any of your passengers have special problems – diabetes or allergy to bee stings, for example – and brush up on first aid for those particular problems.

Your first aid kit should, at very least, contain these items: one 3-inch and one 4-inch Ace wrap, packed in a zippered plastic bag so they stay dry; surgical tape and sterile 2X2s; band-aids; antiseptic; space blanket; triangular bandage; GI surplus 3-inch or 4-inch pressure bandage (or, alternatively, a feminine hygiene pad, which can be used with an Ace Wrap to make a pressure bandage); scissors; tweezers; 6 safety pins; and a flashlight.

Safety Equipment Checklist:
- at least one spare oar
- at least one spare oarlock
- at least one spare drain plug
- 100 feet of soft (cotton or nylon) rope, to use if lining becomes necessary. Soft rope is more expensive than hemp or plastic but is easier on your hands.
- a small plastic bucket for bailing
- a large sponge (makes a better bailer if the water is less than an inch deep).
- a boat puncture repair kit (which, for day trips, will probably consist of a roll of duct tape)
- one lifejacket, in good condition, for each person on board
- at least one railroad flare for each person on board, taped to lifejackets
- a first aid kit
- raingear (never go anywhere in Oregon without raingear).

Boating Courtesy
Riverboating courtesy should be easy – do unto others as you would have them do unto you – but sometimes it doesn't seem to work out that way. Drift boaters are, for the most part, an easygoing bunch, and discourteous acts are more likely to happen from not knowing any better than from bad intentions. Here are a few suggestions for making the river a more congenial place to be and for making fewer enemies while you're there.

If you are uncertain of the path to follow through rapids, anchor upstream and watch a few boats go through. If, after watching other boats go through, you think you'd still feel more comfortable following another boat, ask permission. Nobody likes to be crowded – if the other oarsman gives you permission to follow him through, give him at least a 25-yard headstart; that puts you close enough to see his maneuvers, but far enough away to give you both plenty of rowing room.

Don't seagull (seagulling is tailgating another angler you think knows more about the river than you, in hopes of learning his fishing secrets).

Don't get caught up in a boat race for the best fishing spots; you'll end up bypassing more good water than you fish. Any given mile of river will have a hundred good spots to fish for salmon or steelhead, and a thousand places to fish for trout. Make a habit of fishing at least one spot you've never fished before, every time you fish a given stretch of river. After a season or two, you'll

Oscar's Rapids is a 4 in difficulty at river stage 1.7 (summer level), when the river log was compiled, but is only a 2+ at river stage 3.0 (winter level), when this picture was taken. As you can see the North Umpqua has much ledge rock with potentially dangerous whitewater chutes.

know enough about the river to find a place to fish at lesure while everyone else is playing riverboat race, and it may give you the edge that puts fish in your boat when everyone else goes home empty-handed.

Other boaters appreciate a little fishing room. If the boat downstream of you is dragging flies or pulling plugs, don't pass it and begin fishing close downstream. If it is anchored, and its occupants are drift fishing, don't float over their drift. If it is holding in an eddy in rapids, fishing the pocket water, try not to crowd it when you pass through the rapids.

Wading anglers appreciate a little river room, too. The whitewater between Boulder Flat and Glide has, over the past few years, gained some renown among rafters and kayakers, and conflicts have developed between the floaters and the waders (this area cannot legally be fished from a boat). Both groups have the right to be there; the conflict is largely manufactured, and is more illusory than real. Floaters have little or no effect on trout fishing. If you are fishing a steelhead hold at sunrise, and a raft floats over the fish, it will spook — but most floaters are not on the water until later in the day. If you are fishing a steelhead hole in one of the more heavily fished sections of the river while the sun is hot on the water, your chances of hooking a fish are poor, and a raft or kayak floating by does not make your effort more of an exercise in futility than it already is.

However, when an angler buys a trip to the North Umpqua to quest after the wily and elusive steelhead, with the idea he is travelling to a pristine wilderness stream untrammelled by humans, only to find himself waded out tail deep to a tall giraffe in icewater and surrounded by kayaks, he becomes understandably agitated.

When passing a wading angler with a boat, raft, or kayak, hold up at least 30 yards upstream, ask the wader where to pass, and don't float over the drift or hold being fished.

Whether they admit it or not, most of the people you see on the river are looking for solitude — and if not for solitude, then at least for something they don't have in their own living room. Let them have it. There are hundreds of places, even on the high-traffic stretches of river, that never get fished. In the middle of summer, when there's a steady stream of boats, rafts, rubber duckies, and kayaks in the main channel of the river, the side channels and backwaters are likely to be deserted. Because so few people use them, these backwaters are likely to produce much of the best fishing. People seem to herd together, even when they profess to be seeking solitude — so if some jerk wants to crowd you out of a particular spot, let him have it. Leave the crowd and do a little bit of exploring, and you may find something better than you'd have believed possible.

If possible, plan your trip for the middle of the week. The river gets most heavily used on Friday afternoon, Saturday, and Sunday. By sundown on Sunday, the fish have had so much tackle flung at them that the slightest disturbance makes them run for cover, wondering what missed them. Give them all of Monday to relax a little, and plan your fishing trip for Tuesday, Wednesday, or Thursday.

Avoid unnecessary noise. Fish live in such a noisy world, with water roaring and rocks rumbling as they roll downstream, that noises boaters make may or may not be noticed. But, whether or not the noise bothers the fish, it bothers the fishermen. If you do a lot of banging around, or play your ghetto blaster at full volume, most fishermen will grit their teeth and do nothing — but there are a few fellows on the river who will decide it's a wonderful excuse for heaving a rock at you.

Be kind to the picnic spots. By midsummer, the more popular lunch stops along the river are likely to be trashed out. The fire rings are full of yesterday's garbage, abuzz with flies. The ground is littered with empty beverage cans and fast-food wrappers. The shoreline is littered with tangles of monofilament line. The surrounding trees are hacked up by folks who think they can burn green wood.

Don't make any new fire rings; if you want to stop at a spot that lacks a fire ring, plan on eating a cold lunch or cooking on a gas campstove.

Either destroy or haul out any plastic trash you create. If you peel a snarl of monofilament line off your reel, either burn it or cut it into short pieces with your pocketknife; long pieces or tangles of monofilament are deadly to small wildlife, especially nesting birds. Ducks and fish strangle themselves on plastic six-pack holders.

Use only dead and down wood for firewood. Green, unseasoned wood doesn't burn very well and is not suitable for cooking. Standing dead trees are an essential part of the ecology of the wild, providing food, or home, or both, to everything from worms to small mammals. Firewood may be scarce at most of the popular camping and picnic areas, so packing a bag of charcoal in the drop-seat of your boat will insure that you have the wherewithal to make a fire at your lunch stop.

Axes can be left at home on day trips; any stick of wood too large to be broken over your knee is too large to use in a cooking fire.

Sanitation

During the time this book was being written, the city of Roseburg accidentally spilled a large volume of raw sewage into the South Umpqua; since the sources of pollution are few, such a catastrophe is not likely on the North Umpqua. Yet, even though the North Umpqua remains an essentially wild river, you should not drink the water unless it has been treated.

Most wild waters in Oregon harbor an intestinal parasite, a protozoan of the *Giardia* genus, which causes dysentery-like symptoms; in addition, the North Umpqua may also be polluted with bacteria from human wastes.

Many camp- and picnic-grounds along the river have potable water supplies; if you plan to stop at a place where no treated water is available, you should either use water brought from a safe source, or treat the wild water before drinking it.

The water can be made safe to drink by treatment with chemicals, or by boiling. Keeping water at a rolling boil for at least 3 minutes will kill dangerous parasites or bacteria, but it also removes all the free oxygen from the water, and makes it taste flat; to re-aerate the water, pour it back and forth between two pots after it cools (water will not hold appreciable amounts of free oxygen at temperatures higher than 90 degrees Fahrenheit). Adding a teaspoon of chlorine bleach or one G.I. surplus water treatment tablet per quart, then allowing the water to sit for half an hour before consumption, should also render the water safe to drink.

Try to leave your lunch spot cleaner than you found it. Carry a heavy duty garbage bag in your boat; after lunch, burn all the paper trash in the area, and carry everything else out with you for deposit in a trash can at the boat landing. Picking up other people's litter and toting it out is a disgusting business, but the only alternative is allowing it to pile up and ruin the river.

If you see someone littering, hacking up a live tree, spray-painting graffiti, or otherwise committing acts of vandalism, stop them if you can — and whether or not they stop, report them to the State Police (1-800-452-7888) or the Douglas County Sheriff's Office (Dial 911).

Although most of the picnic areas along the river have pit toilets, there are few picnic areas along the boatable part of the river — so you should make a stop at a place that has toilet facilities before you go on the river. Carry a small trowel in your boat, so if a nature call is necessary during the day, you can use what backpackers refer to as the "cat method:" dig a small hole for it, and when the deed is did, cover it up.

Carry white toilet paper on the river; the dyes in colored papers can be harmful to the environment.

If you are angling and kill fish, don't throw the entrails in the river; butcher the fish at a boat landing or campground and dispose of the entrails in a garbage can.

The river's ability to cleanse itself is phenomenal, but the river, like everything else in nature, will die if subjected to too large a dose of the human species.

Chapter 8

FISHING the LOWER RIVER

Caution: The following river drifting information is not absolutely accurate due to on-going changes in the river caused by high water, such as placement of dangerous logs and sweepers and the movement of rocks and channels. Use it only as a general guide and scout all water you are not sure of. You should have substantial river experience before drifting any portions of the North Umpqua!

Access

East of Glide, the country along both banks of the river is publicly owned, and fishing access is assured; west of Glide, almost the entirety of both banks of the river is privately owned and posted, and the only way the river can be fished is either from a boat, or from the bank at the limited access offered by boat landings and parks. The only non-boat-landing access is at Jackson Wayside, on the north bank opposite Whistler's Bend Park.

The drifts covered in this chapter are *Lone Rock* to *Colliding Rivers, Colliding Rivers* to *Whistler's Bend,* and *Amacher Park* to *Hestnes Landing.* The drifts from Whistler's Bend to Winchester Lake, and from Hestnes Landing to River Forks Park are omitted with reason.

The drift from Whistler's Bend to the landing on Page road, at the upper end of Winchester Lake, can be run in a single day, if you row from daylight to dark. However, it is too long to be fished in a single day, and, since all the shoreline between the two landings is privately owned and posted, there is no place to camp and make a two-day drift of the trip. In addition, Dixon Falls, which approximately marks the halfway point between Whistler's Bend and the lake, is a barrier to all but the most experienced boatmen. There are rumors that the State of Oregon is negotiating for access to build boat landings and break this section of river into more digestible drifts, but any concrete action in that direction is probably 2 or 3 years off.

The drift from Hestnes Landing to River Forks is short enough to fish in a single day, but it is a pain in the neck to float; and any time the fishing is good on this lower drift, it will also be good on the Amacher Park to Hestnes Landing run. River Forks Parks offers bank-fishing access to several good salmon, steelhead, and trout fishing holes.

Water Flow Levels

When these river logs were compiled, the North Umpqua River stage reading printed in the Roseburg and Eugene newspapers was 1.7 feet. The whole of Oregon was suffering through the worst drought in at least half a century. Canton Creek, which is usually knee deep and 30 feet wide at its confluence with Steamboat Creek, was a sluggish dribble you could step over. Steamboat Creek was suffering from heat exhaustion and dehydration. Little River was the merest of gravelly trickles. When the first autumn rain finally fell, a few fish drowned because they had forgotten how to behave in water.

Because the water was so low, the river logs should get you through the rapids at any water level. At higher water levels, some of the minor rapids described will disappear; some of the more difficult rapids may become unrunnable or only marginally runnable, and those bad spots will be noted in the logs.

However, having a river log in hand when you drift the North Umpqua does not relieve you of any of your responsibilities as a boatman. You should make an honest appraisal of your skill as an oarsman, and stay away from water you cannot safely run. You should scout every rapid marked "scouting necessary" in the log, and you should scout any place that puzzles you, or where you can't see a clear path all the way through. The floor of the North Umpqua River is mostly bedrock, so the rapids are not likely to change much from movement of the streambed, but any rapids can become occluded if a log washes in from upstream, and going into any rapids blind can put you in deadly danger.

Whitewater Classifications

There is a 6-level International Scale of River Difficulty, which attempts to classify whitewater rapids. The International scale is misleading for drift boaters because it attempts to combine technical difficulty and danger to life and limb, and is not a true gauge of either. For example, in technical difficulty, on a scale of 1 to 6, Oscar's rapids are a 4 or 4+ (depending on water level); but as a danger to life, it may only be a 1+ or 2. On the other hand, Colliding Rivers Falls, which is only a 3 in technical difficulty, is a 5 in danger.

The river logs in this chapter will still use a 1 to 6 rating system, and 1 will still be easy and 6 will still be impossible, but the ratings will describe how difficult a rapid is to negotiate in a drift boat. Any rapids generally considered dangerous, whether easy or difficult to get through, will have **DANGER!** printed next to its difficulty rating, and the danger will be described. When you see **DANGER!**, don't take it lightly.

How to Use the River Logs

These river logs are divided into 3 columns. Here are two sample log entries from the Lone Rock – Colliding Rivers log:

0:15		**INDEX POINT** – passing under the Glide Trestle Bridge.
0:19	3	Rapids. **Identification:** Island on the right. The river splits into 3 channels; use the center channel. Very shallow, swift, steep pouroff. Enter **left** of center, rockpick toward **left** bank as you drop into the middle of the rapids, then rockpick back to the **right** to drop on through the pouroff.

The river logs in some books are marked in river miles – yet few oarsmen have any reliable sense of how long a river mile is. These logs measure distance by the amount of time it takes to travel, and that time is listed in column one. The oarsmen who compiled the logs rowed through flatwater areas; on the flowing stretches of river, they drifted with the current, rowing only as necessary to maneuver through rapids. At water levels higher than 1.7, actual elapsed time will differ from the times in column one, but the logs contain enough index points – fixed, recognizable landmarks – to keep you comfortably aware of your position.

The second column contains a number that rates how difficult a rapid is to negotiate. How those ratings are arrived at is described under "Whitewater Classifications," above.

The third column contains descriptions of rapids and index points, recommendations to the oarsman, and fisherman's information.

Occasionally, you'll find the word "rockpicking" in column 3; this means that there are rocks in the river, and you should be a good enough oarsman not to need a blow-by-blow description of how to miss each one.

Bringing a boat through Colliding Rivers Falls.

RIVER LOG: Lone Rock Slide to Colliding Rivers Ramp

To reach Lone Rock Slide, turn south on Lone Rock Road in downtown Glide. The slide is located just east of mile post 1 on Lone Rock Road.

TIME	RAPIDS	NOTES
hr:min	rating	information
0:00		**Lone Rock Pole Slide**
0:01	1	Minor chute rapids, 75 yards downstream of the landing; stay on the tongue of the pouroff. The tail-out just above the pouroff is good steelhead fishing territory.
0:04	2	Shallow pouroff. Enter near **right** bank, avoid the rock in the middle of the pouroff. This rapid is only a 1+ at higher water levels.
0:07		Entering long stretch of flatwater above Glide Trestle Bridge.
0:14		Good Chinook hole just upstream of the Glide Trestle Bridge. The hole is 25+ feet deep at normal river flow levels; the deepest part of the hole is against the rock ledge on the left.
0:15		**INDEX POINT** – passing under the Glide Trestle Bridge.
0:19	3	Rapids. **Identification:** Island on the right. The river splits into three channels; use the center channel. Very shallow, swift, steep pouroff. Enter **left** of center, rock pick toward **left** bank as you drop into the middle of the rapids, then rockpick back to the **right** to drop on through the pouroff. At higher water levels, there will be 2- to 3-foot-high standing waves at the bottom.
0:20		**INDEX POINT** – On the right, a high gray pumice bluff overlaid with a layer of river gravel. French Creek enters the river at the lower end of the bluff.
0:23	1	Shallow riffle; stay in main current.
0:24	2+	Rapids. Pour-offs over two rock shelves. Enter **left** of center; after passing the first rock shelf, pull back toward the **right** bank. As you approach the second shelf, pull **left** to avoid the waterfalls the shelf causes. This rapid can be mildly dangerous in high water, because the hydraulics tend to push the boat to the right over the falls.
0:27	1+	Bedrock riffle, upper section. Enter on the **right,** stay to the right of the main current.
0:28	1+	Middle section. Riffle has turned to gravel. Work toward the **left** bank, then back to the **right** to drop into the bottom section.
0:29	1	Bottom end. Riffle, stay in **main** current, This riffle will be washed out at higher water levels.
0:33	2	Swift chute riffle. Enter **midstream,** pass **left** of the boulder 20 yards downstream. Because of the hydraulics, this riffle will be a 2+ at higher water levels.
0:35	2+	Shallow, steep, swift pouroff. Enter **midstream,** pull to **right,** then rockpick back to the **left** to exit at bottom.
0:42	1+	Shallow riffle. Upper end: enter near the rocks on the **left,** and rockpick down. Bottom end: pull back a little to the **left** to avoid the rock ledge. At higher water levels, this riffle will have standing waves at the bottom.
0:45	1+	Shallow gravel riffle. Enter **midstream.** The current will drop you through near the rocks on the **left;** pull back just enough to avoid the rocks.

0:46	2	Shallow bedrock riffle. Enter **midstream.** Cross the rock shelf 20 yards downstream next to the boulder that sticks out of the water, and pull back to the **right** bank to exit.
		DANGER: APPROACHING COLLIDING RIVERS FALLS — SCOUTING NECESSARY. Scout from the right bank. **Identification:** Bedrock shelf along right bank; large bedrock island in midstream; downstream, to the left of the island, you can see the Highway 138 concrete bridge over Little River.
0:51	3	**Colliding Rivers Falls.** Set up approximately **midstream** above the point of the island. Drop over the falls next to the **right** bank of the island. Passengers can walk around the falls along the right bank. At high water levels, the hydraulics make the falls unrunnable. The rock island provides a good viewing point for the geological phenomenon called Colliding Rivers, and the gravel bar at the foot of the island is a good picnic spot. Colliding Rivers Park is on the left bank above the island, and the land below the falls on the right is privately owned and posted.
0:56	1	Gravel pouroff downstream of the island. Stay on the **tongue** of the current.
0:57	1+	Bedrock pouroff. Run near the **left** bank, and don't be surprised when your boat bangs the rock at the bottom.
1:01		**Colliding Rivers Boat Ramp on left bank.**

Colliding Rivers, where the North Umpqua meets the Little River, 1953. Douglas County Museum photo

RIVER LOG: Colliding Rivers Boat Ramp to Whistler's Bend Park

Colliding Rivers Boat Ramp is an improved boat ramp adjacent to Highway 138 approximately one-tenth mile west of Colliding Rivers Park.

TIME hr:min	RAPIDS rating	NOTES information
0:00		**Colliding Rivers Boat Ramp.** The Colliding Rivers Hole, adjacent to the boat ramp, is an excellent salmon and steelhead hole.
0:03	1	300 yards downstream of the boat ramp. Shelf rock riffle. Enter and run approximately **midstream.** The rocky area upstream and to the left of the riffle is superb trout fly fishing water.
0:05	2+	Steep, shallow, swift riffle. Enter at **midstream,** and rockpick down through, missing the boulder sticking up about halfway down the rapids. Exit to **left** of center.
0:06		At the bottom end of the rapids, a good Chinook fishing hole.
0:10		Flat water stretch above the North Bank Road Bridge.
0:22		**INDEX POINT** – passing under the North Bank Road Bridge.
0:24	1+	The river splits into several channels around bedrock outcrops. Use the largest channel, which is to the **left** of center.
0:25	2+	Rapids, 125 yards downstream of bridge. Enter in channel closest to **left** bank, between rocks. Rockpick through to the bottom. In higher water, this rapid is only a 1+.
0:29		**INDEX POINT** – at the bottom end of a chute, a rock island with one lone dwarf tree. Go **left** of the island. This area is called the Rock Garden, and is a productive fishing area.
0:35	1+	**Santos Rapids,** a series of shallow gravel riffles. Enter and run near the **right** bank. The gravel beds in this section of river are spawning redds for Chinook. The hole below the rapids is a good Chinook and steelhead fishing hole.
0:42	1	Gravel riffle. Enter one third off **left** bank, and stay in the main current down through.
0:49		**INDEX POINT** – the river splits into channels around 2 islands; use the **right** channel.
0:49	1+	Gravel riffle. Rockpick through about one third out from the head of the island. The island is a popular picnic or rest stop.
0:50	1	Gravel riffle at the bottom end of the island. Stay in the main current along the **left** bank.
0:52		Flatwater stretch below the islands.
0:56		**INDEX POINT** – powerline crosses the river overhead.
1:03		**INDEX POINT** – At the bottom end of the flat water, there is a rock garden all the way across the river.
1:03	1+	**Robbi's Chute Rapids.** Enter one third out from the **right** bank, down the wide chute with a boulder sticking up in the middle of it 20 yards downstream. Drift straight downstream past the boulder to set up for Oscar's Rapids.
1:05	4	**Oscar's Rapids.** After dropping through Robbi's Chute, rockpick **left** to approximately **midstream.** The rapid pours over several rock and gravel shelves; rockpick down through the shelves at about midstream, until you near the last shelf and can see calmer

		water downstream. At that last rock shelf, follow the chute on the **right** side of the shelf.
1:08		The hole at the bottom of Oscar's Rapids is called Oscar's Hole, and is a good spot for baitfishing for Chinook (the current is too roily and unpredictable for pulling plugs).
1:09	1+	**Knight's Rapids.** Riffly chute through the bedrock; enter and run along the **right** bank.
1:10	2+	**Small waterfall.** Enter along the **left** shore of the hummock island with dwarf trees on it; rockpick down the channel, and drop over the falls to the **left** of the main current, to avoid the suckhole behind a boulder at the bottom of the falls.
1:11	1	**INDEX POINT** – 50 yards downstream of the falls, the river splits into several channels through bedrock; stay in the **main channel,** approximately midstream.
1:12	1+	Pour-off at the bottom end of the channel; stay **midstream.**
1:13	3+	**Five-Slot Rapids,** so named because the river splits into five slots through the bedrock. At low water levels, all the way through the rapids, you will be rockpicking through extremely tight spots and banging your oars against rocks. At higher water levels, there is more room to maneuver, and Five-Slot would rate only a 3. At higher water levels, the channel to the far **left** can be run. At low water, use the **second channel from the right.** After dropping over the first pouroff, ferry **left** and drop through the midstream slot, and run it touching-close to the **right** side of the boulder in the middle of the slot.
1:15		Exit Five-Slot into a fishing hole called The Flat.
1:17	1	**Shallow riffle.** Run the **left** channel.
1:18	1+	**Pouroff. Use the second channel** over from the **right** bank. Drop over the pouroff to the **left** of the boulder in mid-channel. Good fishing hole downstream of the rapids.
1:20	3	**The Esses Rapids.** Rockpicking in tight quarters and difficult hydraulics. Enter next to the **right** bank, **go left** of the boulder, then rockpick down the slot along the **right** bank. Drop over the pouroff and pull **left** of the rock hummock directly downstream. The river splits into two narrow channels; use the **left channel.** The first calm water below The Esses is called the Bait Hole.
1:23	1	**Rock Garden Rapids.** Use the channel along the **right** bank.
1:27	1+	**Whitey's Riffle.** 100 yards of shallow gravel and bedrock riffle; run where the most water shows.
1:29		**INDEX POINT** – a single-strand electric cable crosses the river in the middle of a long flat water stretch. The fishing hole at the lower end of the flat water is called the A-Frame Hole.
1:33	2+	Steep pouroff rapids. Rockpick down the **middle,** where the most water is; go over the pouroff far enough to the **right** to avoid the boulder at the bottom.
1:34	1+	40 yards downstream from the last pouroff, a narrow chute and pouroff. Run **mid-channel.** The hole below the pouroff is a good steelhead fishing spot.
1:37		**INDEX POINT** – as you pass under electric power lines on a stretch of flat water, there is a bald knob hill on your right.
1:38	1	**Upper Merriman Rapids.** Enter the chute on the **right.** the hole below the chute, and above Merriman Rapids, is a good steelhead

fishing spot.

1:39	1+	**Merriman rapids.** Stay in the **main current**, near the **right** bank. The hole below Merriman rapids is called Merriman Hole, and is good steelhead and Chinook holding water. As you drop into Merriman Hole, you will have a high rock bluff with one lone tree on top on your right.
1:46		The hole at the bottom end of the flat water below Merriman rapids is called the Wooden Indian Hole.
1:46	1+	**Wooden Indian Rapids.** Enter near the **left** bank, ferry toward the gravel bar on the **right,** and drop over the second pouroff about midstream.
1:50	1	**Shallow riffle;** run **midstream.**
1:50		**INDEX POINT** – high, wooded rock bluff on the left, gravel bar on the right, and the river dog-legs to the right below the gravel bar.

DANGER: APPROACHING WHISTLER'S FALLS. SCOUTING NECESSARY. Scout from the island in midstream. **Identification:** Wooded island in midstream. Two high rock points 100 yards apart on right bank.

1:55	4	**Whistler's Falls.** Run to the **right** of the island. In high water, the channel to the **left** of the island is boatable, and some hardy souls run the falls along the right bank. In low water, set up by rockpicking down just to the right of the point of the island, and drop over the falls 15 feet from the right shore of the island.
2:00	1	**Bedrock Chute** at bottom end of island. Enter along the **midstream** tongue, and pull **right** to avoid rocks. The hole below the chute is good steelhead holding water.
2:01	2	Continuous minor rapids from the bottom end of the island to Whistler's Bend Boat Ramp.
2:13		**Whistler's Bend Boat Ramp on left bank.**

Whistler's Falls is a very challenging piece of white water where precision oarsmanship is a necessity.

RIVER LOG: Amacher Park to Hestnes Landing

To reach Amacher Park Boat Landing, Take exit 129 from Interstate Highway 5; cross the North Umpqua on the U.S. Highway 99 bridge, and turn right into Amacher Park at the south end of the bridge.

Every gravel bar along this run is a Chinook spawning redd. Make the run any time between late September and the end of October if you want watch Chinook spawning.

TIME	RAPIDS	NOTES
hr:min	rating	information
0:00		**Amacher Park Boat Landing.** Steelhead hold along the rock ledge about 40 feet out abreast of the landing, and around the submerged boulders at the bottom end of the hole.
0:04	2	The river splits into several channels around the bedrock; use the **second channel** from the **right bank.** Rockpicking in very tight quarters. At higher water levels, this rapids is only a 1+.
0:05		The hole at the bottom of the chutes is productive salmon and steelhead water; the fish hold around the submerged boulders in the middle of the hole, and early mornings and late evenings, across the tail-out.
0:09	2	**Pouroff.** Enter **midstream,** and as the boat drops over the pouroff, pull **right** to avoid the boulder at the bottom. The hole below the pouroff is a good Chinook bait or spinner hole; the current is too roily for plug fishing.
0:12	1	**Bedrock riffle.** The channel splits around a boulder in midstream; go **either** side. Steelhead will hold on the upstream side of the boulder.
0:16	1+	**Shallow gravel riffle** about 200 yards long. This riffle disappears at higher water levels. The left half of the river percolates through rock hummocks, and the main force of the river goes down the gravel riffle along the right half of the river. Stay close to the rocks along the **left** side of the gravel riffle. The eddies around the rocks in this gravel riffle are good cutthroat water.
0:20	1	At the bottom end of the gravel riffle, the river funnels down into a bedrock chute. The long, deep slot at the bottom of the chute is good plug fishing water.
0:25	1	**Bedrock pouroff.** Stay in the main current on the **right.**
0:27	1+	Entering a rocky stretch of water about a quarter of a mile long. Some rockpicking is necessary; main flow of the river is along the **right.**
0:33	1	Submerged rock shelf across the channel. Stay in the **main current.** Good Chinook hold just downstream of the rock shelf.
0:34	2	50 yards downstream of the submerged rock shelf, the main current zigzags to the **left** around a cluster of rock hummocks in midstream, then back to the **right** downstream of the rock hummocks. Much rockpicking in shallow water is required. This stretch is all good trout fly fishing water, and is only a 1+ in difficulty at higher water levels.
0:38		Flat water. The main channel of the river has moved to the left bank. The crevices and cracks in the bedrock along the right bank are excellent cutthroat water.
0:40	2+	Entering a 200 yard-long stretch of rapids at bottom end of the flat

water. Enter on **left** side of the river. Rockpick back, over the next 75 yards, to the **right** side of the river, then rockpick down the right bank. Bottom end: rockpick down through the narrow chute along the **right** bank, and exit the rapids into a calm pool about 50 yards square. Salmon and steelhead both hold in this calm pool to rest up from moving through the rapids downstream.

0:46   1   **INDEX POINT** – At the bottom end of the calm pool, there is a rock shelf almost all the way across the river; drop through the chute next to the **left** bank. This chute is at the top end of the river's right-angle curve to the left.

0:48   2+   Rapids right on the bend of the river. At higher water levels, this rapids can be run next to the **left** bank; but in low water, must be run to **right** of center. Enter to the **right** of center, and rockpick down through toward the right bank.

0:49   1   For the next several hundred yards, you will be drifting down through a series of flatwaters and pouroffs. The deep holes along this stretch are good Chinook fishing water.

0:58   1+   **Pouroff.** The main volume of the river pours over a rock garden into a deep hole on the right. Take your boat down the shallow gravel riffle on the **left.**

0:59   1   The last quarter-mile of the drift is a series of holes and breaks; the path across the breaks is obvious; stay in the **main current.** Most of the breaks disappear at higher water levels.

1:05   **Chris Hestnes Boat Landing on the right.**

Jay Baker caught this 32-inch summer steelhead hen on an 8-ounce Sneak. Bill Nuckoll photo

Chapter 9

HIGHWAY LOGS

The North Umpqua River is accessed via Highway 97 and Highway 138 from the east, and Interstate Highway 5 and Highway 138 from the west (Highway 200 – which meets Interstate 5 at the Wilbur exit, 2.5 miles north of Winchester Dam – parallels the North Umpqua and joins Highway 138 a mile west of Glide). These highway logs can be used when traveling in either direction: the mileages eastbound along Highway 138 are given according to the mileposts on that highway (**and those mileposts are not all precisely one mile apart**); the mileages in the other logs are given from zero to end eastbound in the left-hand column, and zero to end westbound in the right-hand column.

FORKS PARK TO HIGHWAY 138 JUNCTION

MILE EAST	MILE WEST	DESCRIPTION
0.0	12.6	**River Forks Park** at the confluence of the north and South Umpqua Rivers (see Ch. 11)
0.8	11.8	Intersection of River Forks Park Road and Douglas County Road 6
1.5	11.1	Milepost 6, Route 6
2.4	10.2	Junction with Douglas County Road 31-A
3.0	9.6	Intersection with Del Rio Road
3.9	8.7	**Chris Hestnes Landing** (see Ch. 11)
7.1	5.5	Roseburg Rod & Gun Club
7.4	5.2	Cross Interstate 5 Freeway (exit 129), junction with U.S. Highway 99.
7.6	5.0	**Winchester Dam** – (see Ch. 12)
7.8	4.8	**John P. Amacher Park** (see Ch. 11)
7.8	4.8	Winchester, Oregon city limits
7.8	4.8	To reach the boat landing on the Winchester impoundment, turn east (upriver) on Page Road; the boat landing is just past milepost 1. It is unimproved and suitable only for use by non-motorized craft.
10.9	1.7	Roseburg, Oregon city limits
2.6	0.0	Junction with Oregon Highway 138

HIGHWAY 138
From the Highway 99 Junction to Lemolo Junction

0.0	72.7	**Junction, Highways 99 and 138**
11.7	61.0	**Whistler's Bend Park** – (see Ch. 11)

MILE EAST	MILE WEST	DESCRIPTION
15.9	56.8	**Colliding Rivers Boat Ramp**
16.2	56.5	Glide, Oregon; **Colliding Rivers Park** – (see Ch. 11)
16.4	56.3	Umpqua National Forest, Glide Ranger Station
17.7	55.0	Glide trestle bridge
19.0	53.7	**The Narrows**
21.0	51.7	Idleyld Park, Oregon
21.2	52.5	**The Narrows Park** – (see Ch. 11)
22.0	50.7	**Swiftwater Park** – (see Ch. 11)
22.2	50.5	Cross Rock Creek, **Rock Creek Fish Hatchery** on left (see Ch. 12). Turn up Rock Creek Road to reach **Rock Creek** and **Mill Pond Recreation Sites** (see Ch. 11)
22.4	50.3	Angling deadline (Lower boundary of the fly fishing only section of the river)
22.9	49.8	**Richard Baker Memorial County Park** – (see Ch. 11)
23.2	49.5	**Mill Creek County Park** – (see Ch. 11)
24.4	48.3	**Unnamed County Park** (see Ch. 11)
25.0	47.7	**Unnamed County Park** (see Ch. 11)
27.1	45.6	**Smith Springs Park** – (see Ch. 11)
28.4	44.3	Trailhead, Susan Creek Trail (see Ch. 12)
29.0	43.7	**Susan Creek Campground** – (see Ch. 11)
30.4	42.3	**Umpqua National Forest Boundary**
32.4	40.3	**Fall Creek Falls Trail**
33.8	38.9	Junction with Wright Creek Road
34.7	38.0	**Bogus Creek Campground** – (see Ch. 11)
38.8	33.9	**Steamboat Creek.** Turn north on Steamboat Creek Road to reach **Scaredman Creek** and **Canton Creek campgrounds** (see Ch. 11)
39.0	33.7	**Mott Trail** (No. 1414) Parking – (see Ch. 7)
39.7	33.0	**Island Campground** – (see Ch. 11)
43.2	29.5	**Apple Creek Campground** – (see Ch. 11)
46.2	26.5	**Horseshoe Bend Campground** – (see Ch. 11 and Ch. 7)
47.0	25.7	Dry Creek (see Ch. 7)
50.4	22.3	**Eagle Rock Campground** – (see Ch. 11 and Ch. 7)
50.9	21.8	Junction with Copeland Creek Road (see Ch. 7)
52.0	20.7	**Boulder Creek Campground** – (see CH. 11 and Ch. 7)
53.2	19.5	Angling deadline – upper limit of the Fly Fishing Only section of river (see Ch. 7)
54.0	18.7	Soda Springs Reservoir (see Ch. 6 and Ch. 12)
58.6	14.1	Toketee Junction (From Glide to Toketee Junction, Highway 138 has paralleled the North Umpqua River; at Toketee, the North Umpqua veers north away from the highway, and from Toketee to Clearwater Falls the highway parallels the Clearwater River. See Ch. 6 and Ch. 7).
65.7	7.0	**Whitehorse Falls Campground** – (see Ch. 11 and Ch. 7)
67.0	5.7	Stump Lake (see Ch. 6 & 7)
69.5	3.2	**Clearwater Falls Campground** – (see Ch. 11 and Ch. 7)

72.7	0.0	Lemolo Junction: turn north on Forest Road 2610 to the Lemolo Lake area (see Ch. 6 & 7), and to reach the junction with Forest Road 3401 (the Thorn Prairie Road, which parallels the North Umpqua from Lemolo Lake to Toketee Lake); continue eastward to **Thielsen Campground**, and to Diamond Lake and Crater Lake National Park.

NORTH UMPQUA RIVER
Kelsay Camp to Toketee Junction

MILE EAST	MILE WEST	DESCRIPTION
0.0	21.1	**Toketee Junction** (Highway 138 mile 58.6 and Forest Road 34)
0.3	20.8	**Toketee Falls Trail** (see Ch. 12)
1.4	19.7	**Toketee Lake Campground** (see Ch. 11 and Ch. 6 & 7)
2.4	18.7	Turn right on Forest Rd. 3401 (Thorn Prairie Rd.) Continue on Road 34 to Reach **Lemolo Forebay** No. 2 (see Ch. 6 and Ch. 11)
3.1	18.0	Trail 1414, Umpqua Warm Springs Segment; bridge across the river.
4.4	16.7	Umpqua Warm Springs trail head and footbridge (see Ch. 12) 12)
7.7	13.4	Thorn Prairie (see Ch. 10)
14.7	6.4	Turn left on Forest Road 2610 (turn right for **Poole Creek Campground** – see Ch. 11 – or to reach Highway 138 at Lemolo Junction.
15.6	5.5	Lemolo Dam; turn right on Forest Road 999 (turn left for **Lemolo Forebay** No. 1 and access to the 4 miles of river immediately downstream of Lemolo Dam – (see Ch. 6 & 7)
16.2	4.9	**Bunker Hill Campground** (see Ch. 11)
17.9	3.2	Junction with Spur Road 400 (turn south to reach **Inlet** and **East Lemolo** campgrounds – see Ch. 11)
19.3	1.8	Junction (fork) with Forest Road 60; bear left onto Road 60, then bear right onto Spur Road 958, the Kelsay Valley Road.
21.1	0.0	**Kelsay Camp**

Chapter 10

A QUICK TOUR of the NORTH UMPQUA'S PEOPLE and PLACES

Umpqua is an Indian word which means "Thundering Water." The Indian population in the land of the thundering waters was composed of groups somewhat isolated from each other by the roughness of the country. The Yoncallas lived in the high country from Elk Creek eastward to the upper Steamboat Creek and coast fork Willamette drainage; the Kalawatsets lived on the coastal end of the Umpqua and Smith rivers; the Umpquas lived along the mainstem of the Umpqua River and up the lower stretches of the North Umpqua; the southern band of the Molalla lived on the west slope of the Cascades, and the Klamath lived on the east slope. Because of the isolation, they developed different languages, but their cultures were similar.

The individual tribes were mostly smaller bands made up of extended family groups. They lived by hunting and fishing, and by gathering nuts, berries, and roots. The women did most of the gathering, and the men did the hunting and fishing. The women, for example, made the spears the men used to fish for salmon. The spear was a straight pole about 12 feet in length, with a sharpened, fire-hardened point on the small end. The man waded into the river with the spear, speared the salmon and pushed the pole up to the bank in a continuous movement — so the fish couldn't wriggle off — and when the fish was in shallows, the woman grabbed it by the gills and carried it ashore.

These Indians had a well-established trade among themselves, and, later, to communicate with white settlers, they spoke Chinook jargon, a trading language that was to the Pacific Northwest what Pidgin English was to the Orient.

Illahe is a corruption of the Chinook jargon word *illahehk*, which means "place" or "land." Illahe Flat, which was once called Caps Illahe, was a rendezvous spot used by several tribes for games, horse racing, and trading fairs. Early travelers wrote about the throngs of people milling about, the excitement of the Indian's horse races and gambling, and of seeing fur peltry for trade stacked higher than a man's head.

The Umpquas and Molallas were not particularly warlike, but measles, chickenpox, and other diseases accepted as an annoying, but seldom fatal fact of life by European explorers, were almost uniformly fatal to them; compared to other areas, the North Umpqua had a sparse native population, and thus, by the turn of the 20th century, most were gone. The few who remained had no reservation land and either lived as dispossessed squatters on federal lands, or as beggars.

A few geographic features are named after Indians. Mace Mountain is named after Mace Tipton, the man called "the last of the Umpquas"; Limpy was the name of one of the final few Indians on the North Umpqua, and several places are named after him.

Many places have Chinook jargon names, but not all of the names were applied by Indians. *Illahe, Lemolo, Toketee, Yakso,* and *Tipsoo* are all Chinook jargon words. The origin of *Illahe* has already been described. *Lemolo* means "wild" and was applied first to a waterfall, and later to the reservoir near the waterfall. *Toketee* means "pretty" or "graceful." *Tipsoo* can mean either "grass" or "hair" (as in the hair on fur peltry). *Yakso* means "hair of the head." Maidu Lake is the source of the North Umpqua River, and according to Lewis A. McArthur's *Oregon Geographic Names*, was named after a tribe of northern California Indians.

The place names and the signs of habitation at Dog Creek, Medicine Creek, and a few other spots, are about all that is left to show there once were Indians along the North Umpqua.

Fur trappers and mountain men were roaming through the country along the lower end of the Umpqua as early as the 1820s, and a few permanent white settlers were showing up by the 1850s, but the North Umpqua remained wild, remote country until well into the 20th century.

Most of the early settlers above Rock Creek were gold miners. The Steamboat Creek drainage and the North Umpqua as high as Boulder Flat were well worked over by gold prospectors, but very few found enough gold to hold their interest. Steamboat is a miner's term: if a mine is played out, it is said to be steamboated;

Zane Grey fly fishing, North Umpqua River. Douglas County Museum photo

likewise, if a miner salts a claim and sells it to a tenderfoot, the tenderfoot is steamboated.

A prospector named Bohemia Johnson, said to have been on the run from the law on the North Umpqua, traveled up Steamboat Creek and is credited with discovering the Bohemia Mine on the divide between Steamboat Creek and Sharps Creek. The Bohemia Mine was the carrot on a stick that started a gold rush on the upper end of Sharp's Creek and turned Cottage Grove into a boom town — but though Sharp's Creek to the north and the Rogue River to the south both gave up gold, no big strike ever materialized on the North Umpqua.

The few settlers who took up Donation Land Claims above Steamboat were mostly interested in horse ranches. One such settler, Bill Bradley, had the reputation of being something more than just a horse rancher. He homesteaded near Caps Illahe around 1880; Bradley Ridge, Bradley Lake, Bradley Flat, and Bradley's Doghouse all take their name from him.

Bill was usually in trouble with the law; when other people began to take up claims near his, some accused him of shooting their stock or other dirty deeds calculated to make them pull up stakes. Some federal agents accused him of crimes up to and including murder, and the local law was always after him for crimes ranging from horse larceny to game law violations. Bradley's Doghouse was one of his hideouts, a small log and dugout cabin on top of the hill near Bradley Lake on one of his getaway trails over the Calapooiyas.

During a storm in late November, 1909, Perry Wright (another homesteader in the area) and two companions found Bill Bradley partially paralyzed and dying a few hundred yards from his cabin on Bradley Flat. From reading the trail sign, Perry Wright speculated that Bradley had been thrown from his horse and hit his head, and was trying to crawl to the river to drown himself so he wouldn't die slowly.

Perry and his companions went to heroic lengths to get help, but the storm was causing the worst floods in 50 years, and the nearest doctor was more than 50 miles away, in Roseburg. It took 4 days to get the doctor to Bradley's cabin. The doctor pronounced Bradley dead on Thanksgiving Day, November 29th, 1909.

Perry Wright's handwritten account of the death of Bill Bradley is on file in the library at the Douglas County Historical Museum in Roseburg.

Logging didn't become economical on the North Umpqua until the first roads had been built. After the dam was completed at Winchester in the late 1880s, one logging company hired a logging crew from "Back East" experienced at working log rafts, to make a log drive down the North Umpqua, from the logging site near Honey Creek to the Winchester Dam. The easterners said the river was too treacherous and refused the job. A local crew was hired to float the logs downriver; they got the log rafts to the dam, but two members of the crew were drowned in the process. The river broke the flume at the dam, and the logs ended up behind the jetty at Winchester Bay, making the venture a disaster from beginning to end.

Much of the early history of the North Umpqua is a history of the U.S. Forest Service. Forest rangers built most of the early trails and roads, gave many of the topographic features their names, and (until the completion of the road from Rock Creek to Diamond Lake) most of the people who lived along the river worked at least part-time for the Forest Service.

Before the 1890s, the land was open for mining or homesteading claims, but few people ventured upstream of Steamboat. In 1893, the mountainous area on the upper end of the river was withdrawn from homesteading and added to other lands already under federal jurisdiction and named the Cascade Forest Reserve. In 1905, the so-called "Transfer Act" gave jurisdiction over the forest reserves to the Department of Agriculture, and the Forest Service was formed. In 1907, the Umpqua National Forest was established.

Apple Creek got its name from a Forest Service camp cook, who decided to cook dried apples for supper, but didn't take into account the way dried apples swell when soaked in water. He ended up cooking more than the camp could eat, and dumped the leftovers in the creek.

Boundary Creek once marked the boundary of the Umpqua National Forest.

Dread and Terror Ridge got its name from the way forest rangers felt about fighting a fire in the thorn thickets and brush that cover it.

Fish Creek Desert is an arid plateau that lies south of Highway 138 at Toketee Lake. In the late 1920s and early 1930s, a group of settlers who argued the government's right to withdraw the land from homesteading settled on Fish Creek Desert. Some of the squatters were good people, but one of their leaders was a chronic troublemaker. In 1932, a federal court sentenced the instigators of the settlement to various terms in jail, then suspended the sentences on the condition that the men not cross the boundary into the Umpqua National Forest. Most of the settlers were not prosecuted; Fish Creek Desert is aptly named — the altitude is too high and the land too barren for successful farming, and rather than use force to remove the remaining settlers, the Forest Service allowed the inhospitality of the land to do its work.

Thirsty Creek was named by disappointed Forest Service firefighters who needed water to fight a fire, but found the creek had gone dry for the summer.

Fred Asam was District Ranger at the North Umpqua Ranger District from 1921 to 1945, and is responsible for many place names:

– He named Harding Butte for then-president, Warren G. Harding. At Job's Garden, the roughness of the tumbled rock garden there reminded him of the biblical story of Job. Loafer Creek may be an example of his sense of humor; he named it that, he said, because it just loafs along. A Forest Service worker building a trail asked Asam if the job looked okay; he said yes, and named the place OK Butte. Scaredman Creek empties into Canton Creek a few miles up from its confluence with Steamboat Creek, and Asam named it after a party of hunters who wanted to camp along the creek, but were scared off when they heard wolves howling at the moon. Asam was Austrian by birth, and named the butte near Thunder Mountain Blitzen Butte; *blitzen* is the German word for lightning. He named Wild Rose Point, near Illahe, for the profusion of wild roses that grow there.

Several places were either named by or for Perry Wright. Devil's Stairway was originally named Devil's Ladder by Perry Wright, because the area was so difficult to travel through on horseback; the Forest Service changed the name after they completed the Harding Butte Trail. Perry, his wife Jesse, and two dogs were crossing a footlog over the falls at the upper end of a creek; the dogs fell in and had to be fished out below the falls, and the Wrights named the creek Dog Creek. Wright also named Hole in the Ground, a low spot in the topography south of the river near Horseshoe Bend; Thorn Prairie, which is covered with thorn brush; and Perry Butte is named after him.

Other early settlers also had a hand in naming the places along the river. A Mr. Inman began building an amusement park and called it Idleyld Park; when completed, the park had picnic grounds, cabins, overnight camping facilities, a dance hall, and a store. Cavitt Creek and falls are named after a rancher named Bob Cavitt who homesteaded there; a 1936 *Forest Service Recreation Guide* marks the Cavitt Ranch and describes Bob Cavitt as the first white settler in the area. Cavitt liked his solitude; he was a bachelor who lived alone and died alone, and was found dead in his cabin. Winter Knight Camp (misspelled Night on most maps) is a wide spot in the road that follows the river from Toketee to Lemolo Reservoirs; it is named after a man who camped there to hunt each winter. Nobody knows who named the Rolling Grounds, located about 7 miles due south of Toketee Lake. The name is descriptive: pumice dust is a good natural insect repellant, because it clogs up their breathing apparatus; Rolling Grounds is a natural pummy-dust bowl animals in the area used for dust baths.

Hatchery augmentation of fish runs is not a new idea; there have been hatcheries on the North Umpqua

since the turn of the century. In 1899, State Senator A.W. Reed pushed a bill through the state legislature which appropriated $15,000 to build four salmon hatcheries, at least one of which was to be built on the Umpqua. The governor signed the bill into law, and Reed came home to Douglas County to look for a proper site for the new hatchery. He and a county commissioner were floating the river between Winchester Dam and the forks, looking for a place to build the hatchery, when their boat swamped and both drowned.

F.C. Reed of Astoria replaced A.W. Reed in the Senate; he announced that no hatchery would be built that year. In 1900, a site was chosen on the north side of

Fly fishing the North Umpqua River demands much skill — including reading water and long casting as well as strong wading ability. Scott Ripley photo

the river (near the present day location of the hatchery at Rock Creek), and that first hatchery was completed in time to harvest eggs for hatching from the 1900 fall Chinook run.

The next year, 1901, a second hatchery was built near the mouth of Steamboat Creek; this second hatchery collected eggs, and cared for them until just before hatching, then transported them to the first hatchery for hatching and release. In 1903, fire destroyed part of the second hatchery; a replacement facility was constructed a few miles further upstream, and was later abandoned by the state.

Before World War I, the Umpqua system had a native population of anadromous fish, and most of the alpine lakes and glacial cirques were barren. Then, at about the time of the first World War, the State of Oregon began stocking the high lakes in the North Umpqua Drainage with rainbow trout.

On the first leg of those early stocking expeditions, fingerlings were shipped by railroad, in cans, to a railhead on the east side of the Cascade Divide not far from Diamond Lake. The cans were held in racks along the inside walls of a specially built rail car named *The Rainbow*, and the water was mechanically aerated.

At the railhead, the cans were loaded on pack mules, two to a mule, for the final leg of their journey (see photograph). If it took more than a single day's travel to reach the final destination, the muleskinners planned their itineraries so they would be camping next to a stream. The tops of the cans were covered with burlap held in place by rubber bands made from inner tubing; the cans were laid in the stream for the night, top end upstream.

The railroads and mule trains have been replaced by tank trucks and airplanes, and today just about every body of water in the state that doesn't dry up in summer

Stocking Elk Lake. Oregon Fish and Wildlife historic photo

or freeze solid in winter has a resident population of gamefish, maintained by annual stocking. Trout, steelhead, coho salmon, and Chinook salmon are released into the North Umpqua from the hatchery at Rock Creek.

The first road pushed upstream from Lone Rock was a single-lane mud road with turnouts, completed as far as Steamboat in 1926; at about the same time, the Forest Service completed a road from Big Camas to Diamond Lake. The road was finally completed all the way from Lone Rock to Diamond Lake in 1939. Once the road was begun, and tourists began using the river, sport anglers began making their mark on the area.

Clarence Gordon came for the fishing in 1929 and stayed to build an inn at Steamboat; the inn still stands and is marked as Gordon's Inn on some maps.

Jack Hemingway, in his *Misadventures of a Fly Fisherman,* tells of travelling down the first North Umpqua highway, and of hooking his first North Umpqua Steelhead.

Zane Grey and Major Mott were among the more colorful characters who made the annual pilgrimage to the North Umpqua to fish for the summer steelhead.

Zane Grey was a New York City dentist who daydreamed about being a Wild West cowboy, and wrote formula shoot'em up western novels that made him rich and famous. He came west and bought a log cabin at Winkel Bar on the Rogue River.

He was an internationally renowned fisherman; he fished the Rogue and other western rivers for salmon and steelhead, but was equally well-known as a blue water fisherman who quested after marlin; yet it was not he, but his Japanese cook who got fishing holes named after him on the North Umpqua. Grey began fishing the North Umpqua in the summer of 1932, from a camp near the mouth of Williams Creek, downstream of Steamboat. His cook, Takehachi, also wanted to fish, but Grey wanted no competition in the better holes and told Takehachi he must limit his fishing to the water abreast the camp. Most of the regular fishermen on the river liked Takehachi better than they did his boss, and when he caught an occasional fish — and especially on the days when he caught fish and Zane Grey didn't — the story would be passed around and laughed about, and in time the two holes abreast of Zane Grey's camp became known as the Upper and Lower Takehachi.

Zane Grey's last year on the North Umpqua was 1937; that year he had a stroke, and he died in 1939.

Jordan Mott was also a summer fixture on the North Umpqua in the early days and an adventuring rakehell of the old school. He was born the son of a multimillionaire New York industrialist, and earned the nickname "millionaire reporter" when he took a job as a New York City newspaper reporter and rode out to cover his reporting assignments in a chauffeured limousine.

In 1912, while estranged from his wife, he met and fell in love with Mrs. Frances Hewitt Bowne, a light opera singer who was estranged from her husband. Although neither had been divorced, they decided to run away together, and sailed from New York on a tramp steamer.

Mott's father sent an agent to chase him down and convince him to come home; after missing Mott and Mrs. Bowne by a few hours in Gibraltar and and again at Port Said, the agent finally caught up with them in Hong Kong. Mott refused to be sensible and forsake Mrs. Bowne and come home, and his father disinherited him. In the following years, to earn a living, Mott worked odd jobs and Mrs. Bowne sang at concerts.

In 1927, they returned to the United States; during their years abroad, both their spouses had obtained divorces, and in 1928 they married each other in Merced, California. They lived on Santa Catalina Island, in California, and Mott worked as an angling guide during the day and wrote fiction at night. His first novel, *Jules of the Great Love,* was a monetary success, and allowed him to begin spending his summers fishing on the North Umpqua.

He did what few men manage. He lived life on his own terms, and he chose where he would die. He died in his fishing camp near Steamboat on the North Umpqua.

CAMPGROUNDS, PARKS
and PICKNICKING AREAS

OVERVIEW

Douglas County, the U.S. Forest Service, and the Bureau of Land Management all administer developed overnight camping facilities along the North Umpqua. Some are fee areas, charging from $3 to $6 per camping group per night, and some charge extra for more than one vehicle parked at a single campsite.

In addition, there are developed picnic sites every mile or so along the high-use part of the river; these are Day Use Only areas administered by Douglas County.

In the directory that follows, "improved picnic site" means a place supplied with a firepit and picnic table. "Improved campsite" is a place with a firepit, picnic table, and a level spot to pitch a tent or park a recreational vehicle. Potable water is water supplied by the campground's administering authority and assumed to be safe to drink; if you drink untreated water, you run the risk of infestation with intestinal parasites. Most of us know what a flush toilet is; a "pit toilet" is a permanent structure built over a cesspool in a campground, and a "chemical toilet" is a self-contained portable structure of the sort sometimes seen at construction sites.

Rather than listing the recreation sites alphabetically, they are listed in the order most useful to a weary traveller – from the river's confluence to its source, and with location given in reference to the nearest major highway.

If you wish to hire rooms, you can get the addresses and telephone numbers of the resorts along the river from a Douglas County, Oregon, telephone directory, available from your local public library or telephone company.

DISPERSED CAMPING

Dispersed camping areas are wilderness areas or other areas that have traditionally been used as campsites, and which receive considerable use but do not have developed campsites. In such areas, it is usually legal to pick a spot and set up camp – however, because of changes in the level of fire danger, the regulations governing dispersed camping can change daily during the summer, so you should check with the U.S. Forest Service before you pitch your tent.

Since some areas along the North Umpqua are being loved to death, the environment will thank you if you forego "dispersed" camping and camp only in developed campgrounds.

If you do camp outside a developed campground, leave no trace of yourself behind: pack your trash and garbage out, use the "cat" method of sanitation, cook with a white gas or propane stove, and, if you must build a wood fire, don't make any new fire rings.

River Forks Park (Douglas County)

Location: At the confluence the north and south forks of the Umpqua River.

Recreation facilities: A large open recreation and games area, a children's playground, a roofed pavilion, an improved boat landing, and developed picnic sites. Fishing access to the Umpqua river.

Potable water: Yes.

Sanitary facilities: Flush toilets.

Overnight camping: Not allowed.

Chris Hestnes Landing (Douglas County)

Location: 3.5 miles west of I-5 on Del Rio Road.

Recreational facilities: Developed boat landing and picnicking area. Fishing access to the North Umpqua River (see Ch. 8).

Potable water: No. Untreated water is available from the river.

Sanitary facilities: Chemical toilet.

Overnight camping: Not allowed.

John P. Amacher Park (Douglas County)

Location: South shore of the river, adjacent to Highway 99 and exit 129 from Interstate 5.

Recreational facilities: Parking, improved picnic sites, improved boat landing, improved campsites. Fishing access to the North Umpqua River (see Ch. 5, 8, & 12).

Potable water: Yes.
Sanitary facilities: Pit toilets.
Overnight camping: Yes.

Whistler's Bend Park (Douglas County)
Location: Turn left off Highway 138 one-half mile east of milepost 11.
Recreational facilities: Parking area, improved boat landing, 30 improved picnic sites. Fishing access to the North Umpqua River (see Ch. 8).
Potable water: Yes.
Sanitary facilities: Flush toilets.
Overnight camping: 24 improved campsites.

Colliding Rivers Park (USFS)
Location: Adjacent to Highway 138 at milepost 17.
Recreational facilities: Colliding Rivers Park is in the town of Glide, Oregon, and next door to the North Umpqua USFS Ranger District offices. It has historical, geological, and botanical information markers, and an improved picnic area (see Ch. 8, 10, & 12).
Potable water: No.
Sanitary facilities: Pit toilet.
Overnight camping: Not allowed.

The Narrows Park (Douglas County)
Location: Adjacent to Highway 138 just east of milepost 21.
Recreational facilities: 6 improved picnic sites. Fishing access to the North Umpqua River (see Ch. 6).
Potable water: No. Untreated water is available from the river.
Sanitary facilities: Pit toilets.
Overnight camping: Not allowed.

Swiftwater Park (Douglas County)
Location: Turn south from Highway 138 across the bridge at milepost 22.
Recreational facilities: Six improved picnic sites. Fishing access to the North Umpqua River (see Ch. 6).
Potable water: Yes.
Sanitary facilities: Flush toilets.
Overnight camping: Not allowed.

Rock Creek Recreation Area (BLM)
Location: Turn north from Highway 138 on Rock Creek Road (.2 miles east of milepost 22), and drive approximately 7.5 miles.
Recreational facilities: Improved picnic and camping sites, and playground.
Potable water: Yes.
Sanitary facilities: Pit toilets.
Overnight camping: Yes.

Mill Pond Recreation Site (BLM)
Location: Turn North from Highway 138 on Rock Creek Road (.2 miles East of milepost 22), and drive approximately 6 miles.
Recreational facilities: Improved picnic and camping sites, playground, camp host.
Potable water: Yes.
Sanitary facilities: Pit toilets.
Overnight camping: Yes.

Richard Baker Memorial County Park (Douglas County)
Location: Off Highway 138, .1 mile west of milepost 23.
Recreational facilities: 25 improved picnic sites. Fishing access to the North Umpqua River (see Ch. 6).
Potable water: Yes.
Sanitary facilities: Pit toilets.
Overnight camping: Not allowed.

Mill Creek County Park (Douglas County)
Location: Off Highway 138, .2 miles east of milepost 23.
Recreational facilities: Improved picnic sites. Fishing access to the North Umpqua River (see Ch. 6).
Potable water: No, untreated water is available from the river.
Sanitary facilities: Pit toilet.
Overnight camping: Not allowed.

Unnamed Picnic Area (Douglas County)
Location: Off Highway 138, .4 miles east of milepost 23.
Recreational facilities: Improved picnic site. Fishing access to the North Umpqua River (see Ch. 6).
Potable water: No. Untreated water is available from the river.
Sanitary facilities: Pit toilets.
Overnight camping: Not allowed.

Unnamed Picnic Area (Douglas County)
Location: Off Highway 138 at milepost 25.
Recreational facilities: Improved picnic site. Fishing access to the North Umpqua River (see Ch. 6).
Potable water: No. Untreated water is available from the river.
Sanitary facilities: None.
Overnight camping: Not allowed.

Smith Springs Park (Douglas County)
Location: Off Highway 138, .1 mile east of milepost 27.
Recreational facilities: Twelve improved picnic

sites. Fishing access to the North Umpqua River (see Ch. 6).

Potable water: No. Untreated water is available from the river.

Sanitary Facilities: Pit toilets.

Overnight Camping: Not allowed.

Susan Creek Recreation Area (BLM)

Location: Off Highway 138 at milepost 29.

Recreational facilities: Thirty-three campsites for tent or trailer. There is a natural sand beach on the riverbank on the southeast side of the campground. Separate Day Use Only picnicking area. Fishing access to the North Umpqua River. Access to Susan Creek Trail (see Ch. 6 & 12).

Potable water: Yes.

Sanitary facilities: Flush toilets.

Overnight camping: Yes.

Bogus Creek Campground (USFS)

Location: Off Highway 138, .7 miles East of milepost 34.

Recreational facilities: Nine improved picnic sites, five improved tent campsites, and ten improved trailer campsites. Fishing access to the North Umpqua River (see Ch. 6).

Potable water: Yes.

Sanitary facilities: Flush toilets.

Overnight camping: Yes. Fee area.

Scaredman Creek Camp (BLM)

Location: From Highway 138, turn north on Steamboat Creek Road (Forest Road 38) and drive approximately .5 miles to its junction with Canton Creek Road; turn left on Canton Creek Road and drive 3 miles.

Recreational facilities: Improved picnic and camping sites. ∗Special note: The entire Steamboat Creek Drainage (which includes Canton Creek) is closed to all angling. In late winter and early spring, steelhead can be seen spawning in the Scaredman Creek area.

Potable water: Yes.

Sanitary facilities: Pit toilets.

Overnight Camping: Yes.

Canton Creek Campground (USFS)

Location: From Highway 138, turn north on Steamboat Creek Road (Forest Road 38), and drive .2 miles.

Recreational facilities: Eight improved picnic sites.

∗Special note: The entire Steamboat Creek Drainage is closed to all angling.

Potable water: Yes.

Sanitary facilities: Flush toilets.

Overnight camping: Not allowed.

Mott Parking Lot (USFS)

Location: Turn right across the bridge from Highway 138 at mile post 39.

Recreational facilities: Fisherman's parking and fishing access to the North Umpqua River. Access to the Mott Segment of the North Umpqua Trail (see Ch. 6 & 10).

This hatchery origin summer steelhead fell for a weighted spinner. Scott Ripley photo

Potable water: No. Untreated water is available from the river.

Sanitary facilities: None.

Overnight camping: Not allowed.

Island Campground (USFS)

Location: Off Highway 138, .8 miles east of milepost 38.

Recreational facilities: Six improved tent campsites and one improved trailer campsite. Fishing access to the North Umpqua River (see Ch. 6).

Potable water: No. Untreated water is available from the river.

Sanitary facilities: Pit toilets.

Overnight camping: Yes.

Apple Creek Campground (USFS)

Location: Off Highway 138, .4 miles past milepost 42.

Recreational facilities: Six improved tent campsites and two improved trailer campsites. Fishing access to the North Umpqua River. Access to the North Umpqua Trail (see Ch. 6 & 10).

Potable water: No. Untreated water is available from the river.

Sanitary facilities: Pit toilets.

Overnight camping: Yes.

Horseshoe Bend Campground (USFS)

Location: Off Highway 138 about halfway between mileposts 45 and 46.

Recreational facilities: Sixteen improved tent campsites, and eighteen improved trailer campsites. Fishing access to the North Umpqua River (see Ch. 6). Camp host.

Potable water: Yes.

Sanitary facilities: Flush toilets.

Overnight camping: Yes. Fee area.

Eagle Rock Campground (USFS)

Location: Off Highway 138 near milepost 49.

Recreational facilities: Sixteen improved tent campsites, and eight improved trailer campsites. Fishing access to the North Umpqua River (see Ch. 6).

Potable water: Yes.

Sanitary facilities: Pit toilets.

Overnight camping: Yes. Fee area.

Boulder Flat Campground (USFS)

Location: Off Highway 138 near milepost 52.

Recreational facilities: Six improved tent campsites, and five improved trailer campsites. Fishing access to the North Umpqua River (see Ch. 5 & 6).

Potable water: Yes.

Sanitary facilities: Pit toilets.

Overnight camping: Yes.

Toketee Lake Campground (USFS)

Location: Turn north on Forest Road 34 at Toketee Junction; Toketee Lake Campground is off Road 34 at the upper end of Toketee Lake.

Recreational facilities: Thirty-three trailer or tent campsites and an improved boat launching ramp. Fishing access to the North Umpqua River and Toketee Lake. Access to the North Umpqua Trail. Access to the Toketcc Falls Trail (see Ch. 5, 6, 10, & 12). The road through the campground is gravelled, but the pumice dust floats up through the gravel, so camping here is a dusty business during the dry part of the year.

Potable water: No. Untreated water is available from the river.

Sanitary facilities: Pit toilets.

Overnight camping: Yes.

Lemolo Forebay No. 2 (USFS)

Location: Turn north from Highway 138 onto Forest Road 34 at Toketee Junction; drive 4.7 miles and turn left on Forest Road 3402; drive one mile to Lemolo Forebay No. 2.

Recreational facilities: Unimproved campsites. Fishing access to Lemolo Forebay No. 2 reservoir (see Ch. 5 & 6).

Potable water: No. Untreated water is available from the forebay.

Sanitary facilities: Pit toilets.

Overnight camping: Yes.

Watson Falls Picnic Ground (USFS)

Location: Turn south off Highway 138, 2.5 miles east of Toketee Junction, onto Forest Road 37.

Recreational facilities: Picnic grounds, Watson Falls Trail trailhead (see Ch. 12).

Potable water: No. Untreated water is available from the creek.

Sanitary facilities: Pit toilets.

Overnight camping: Not allowed.

Whitehorse Falls Campground (USFS)

Location: Off Highway 138, on the Clearwater River, 8 miles east of Toketee Junction.

Recreational facilities: Five improved tent campsites and four improved picnic sites. Campground is located next to Whitehorse falls. Fishing access to the Clearwater River (see Ch. 6 & 12).

Potable water: Yes.

Sanitary facilities: Pit toilets.

Overnight camping: Yes.

Clearwater Falls Campground (USFS)

Location: Off Highway 138, on the Clearwater River, 3.5 miles west of Lemolo Junction.

Recreational facilities: Ten improved tent camping sites and seven improved picnic sites. Campground is located next to Clearwater Falls. Fishing access to the Clearwater River (see Ch. 6 & 12).

Potable water: No. Untreated water is available from the river.

Sanitary facilities: Pit toilets.

Overnight camping: Yes.

Lemolo Lake Campgrounds (USFS)

There are four campgrounds on Lemolo Lake, all on the road that girds the lake (see Ch. 5, 6, 10, & 12).

Location: To reach Lemolo Lake, turn north off Highway 138 onto Forest Road 2610 at Lemolo Junction. Poole Creek Campground is off Road 2610 4 miles north of Highway 138. To reach east Lemolo Campground, turn east off Road 2610 onto Road 400 (3 miles north of Highway 138), drive 2.6 miles, and turn north onto Spur Road 430. To reach Inlet Campground, turn east from road 2610 onto Road 100, and follow Road 100 to its junction with Road 999. Bunker Hill Campground is located on the north shore of the lake on Road 999, .5 miles southeast of its junction with Road 2610.

Poole Creek Campground

Recreational facilities: Forty-one improved trailer campsites; improved boat launching ramp; swimming area encircled by cable, to keep swimmers safe from boats. Poole Creek is also less than one-quarter mile from Lemolo Resort (a commercial enterprise), which has a general store, gas station, fishing tackle store, and boat rental operation.

Potable water: Yes.

Sanitary facilities: Pit toilets.

Overnight camping: Yes. Fee area.

Bunker Hill

Recreational facilities: Unimproved camping and picnicking area. Unimproved dirt road to the campground.

Potable water: No. Untreated water is available from the lake.

Sanitary facilities: None.

East Lemolo

Recreational facilities: Unimproved campsites. The road to East Lemolo is an unimproved dirt track that could be difficult to negotiate with a camp trailer or motor home.

Potable water: No. Untreated water is available from the lake.

Sanitary facilities: Pit toilets.

Overnight camping: Yes.

Inlet

Recreational facilities: Ten improved tent camping sites, four improved trailer camping sites. The road to Inlet is an unimproved dirt track, and high traffic through the campground during the busy season makes it a dusty place to camp.

Potable water: No. Untreated water is available from the river.

Sanitary facilities: Pit toilets.

Overnight camping: Yes.

Thielsen (USFS)

Location: Off Highway 138, just east of Lemolo Junction.

Recreational facilities: Primitive campsites at the end of a rough road ankle deep in pummy dust.

Potable water: None.

Sanitary facilities: Pit toilets.

Overnight camping: Yes.

Kelsay Valley (USFS)

Location: Take Forest Road 999 to its junction with Forest Road 60 (a fork in the road); veer left on Road 60, then immediately turn right on Spur Road 958, the Kelsay Valley Road. Kelsay Valley Road dead-ends at Kelsay Campground and the trailhead for the Maidu Lake segment of the North Umpqua Trail.

Recreational facilities: Spur road 958 into Kelsay Camp is an unimproved dirt track, but the road within the campground has been gravelled to cut down the dust. Kelsay Camp gets heavy use from folks who travel Maidu Lake trail on horseback, and is designed to accommodate horse packers. There is no loading chute, but some campsites have adjacent stall-sized corrals for pack stock. Fishing access to Lake Creek and Lakes Maidu and Lucile (see Ch. 5, 6, 10, & 12).

Potable water: No. Untreated water is available from the creek.

Sanitary facilities: Pit toilets.

Overnight camping: Yes.

Wolf Creek Campground and Picnic Area (USFS)

Location: .4 miles east of milepost 16, turn south from Highway 138 onto the Little River Road; drive 10.8 miles.

Recreational facilities: Three improved tent camping sites, five improved trailer camping sites, thirty improved picnic sites, including group picnicking sites. Children's playground. Fishing access to the Little River. Access to the Wolf Creek Trail. (see Ch. 6 & 12)

Potable water: Yes.

Sanitary facilities: Flush toilets.
Overnight camping: Yes.

Emile Creek (BLM)

Location: .4 miles east of milepost 16, turn south from Highway 138 onto Little River Road; drive 14.9 miles.

Recreational facilities: Six improved campsites (including one group campsite). Improved picnic area. Fishing access to the Little River (see Ch. 6).

Potable water: Yes. Pitcher pump.
Sanitary facilities: Pit toilets.
Overnight camping: Yes.

Coolwater Camp (USFS)

Location: .4 miles·east of milepost 16, turn south from Highway 138 onto Little River Road; drive 16.9 miles.

Recreational facilities: Seven improved tent campsites. Fishing access to the Little River (see Ch. 6).

Potable water: Yes. Pitcher pump.
Sanitary facilities: Pit toilets.
Overnight camping: Yes.

White Creek Camp (USFS)

Location: .4 miles east of milepost 16, turn south from Highway 138 onto Little River Road; drive 17.5 miles.

Recreational facilities: Improved campsites. Fishing access to the Little River (see Ch. 6).

Potable water: Yes. Pitcher pump.
Sanitary facilities: Pit toilets.
Overnight camping: Yes.

Lake-in-the-Woods (USFS)

Location: .4 miles east of milepost 16, turn south from Highway 138 onto Little River Road; drive 26.3 miles.

Recreational facilities: Lake-in-the-Woods was once a major stopping place for travelers through the mountains; there remains a log cabin that travellers used for shelter, and the campground surrounds a lake that the Oregon Department of Fish & Wildlife has stocked with trout. Lake-in-the-Woods has eleven improved tent campsites, and six improved picnic sites. It offers fishing access to Little River and Hemlock Creek, and access to Yakso Falls and Hemlock Falls trails (see Ch. 5 & 6).

Potable water: Yes. Pitcher pump.
Sanitary facilities: Flush toilets.
Overnight camping: Yes. Fee area.

The Colliding Rivers area. Little River enters from the left foreground, the North Umpqua enters from the right; Colliding Rivers Falls is at the upstream (right) end of the island.

Chapter 12

SIDETRIPS

(Diversions for the Days when Fishing is Lousy)

There are people who live, eat, and breathe fishing, who would spend a week on the North Umpqua doing nothing but fishing from daybreak to dark of night, regardless of the weather, regardless of the fishing. They are not usually happy souls — when seen on the river, they are more likely to wear looks of grim determination than smiles.

This chapter is for those of you who fish for fun, who can see beauty in a river beyond the fish it might produce, who might occasionally take a siesta during the heat of the day, and who might feel like taking a break from the fishing once or twice a week to do something else.

What follows are sights and scenery which are well worth the trouble it takes to see them, which range from mildly interesting to intoxicating, and which are either free or priceless, depending on how you look at it.

HIKING

There are several hundred miles of hiking trails in the North Umpqua Corridor. One trail gives access to a natural hot spring; others give access to natural wonders; still others, described in another chapter, offer access to the best fishing.

Hiking trails give you access to wilderness — a place where you can escape the sight, smell, and noise of the rest of humanity. They also give you the chance to watch other worlds, like the closed cosm of nymphal insects hunting minnows or other insects on a rock in the verge of the river.

The wild rhododendrons that bloom in the spring along the trails are famous, but rhododendrons are only one of several hundred species of wildflowers that will bloom in the mountains around the North Umpqua; some will bloom in the snow, some bloom in the hot hillside sun of June. After the flowers bloom, the fruit ripens. There are more than a dozen species of edible berries growing along the river and in the mountains around it, and some have better flavor than anything that can be bought in a grocery store. There are also several plants that have edible roots, stems, leaves, bulbs, or nuts, or are considered medicinal to some degree.

People tend to look at hiking trails the same way they look at roads, as places having little interest except as a way to get from one place to another. Whatever your reason for being in the woods — fishing or otherwise — if you spend a little time each day doing nothing but looking, you'll see that isn't true.

THE TRAILS FROM ILLAHE FLAT

DRY CREEK ROAD — Forest Road 4760 — turns north from Highway 138 near Dry Creek Store, and gives access to several of the better hiking trails. Be sure to take along your camera.

ILLAHE FLAT TRAIL is a moderately steep trail that begins on spur Road 039 off Road 4760; it curves down to the river and passes under Eagle Rock, Old Man Rock, and Old Woman Rock, then climbs up the hill to connect with the Boulder Creek Trail below Pine Bench. At the junction, you may either turn north, to hike another 10 miles through Boulder Creek Wilderness and come out on Road 3810 near Fuller Lake, or turn east and come out on spur Road 012 off Road 4775 below Soda Springs Dam.

ILLAHE LOOKOUT TRAIL is a steep trail that can be hiked from either end; the lower junction is on Road 4760, and the upper junction is on spur Road 100 about a mile off Road 4760.

WILD ROSE TRAIL crosses the divide between the North Umpqua and upper Steamboat Creek drainages; it shares a trailhead with the upper end of the Illahe Lookout Trail on spur Road 100. The trail is about 2 miles long and steep; it passes below Harding Butte, across Wild Rose Point, traverses Devil's Stairway and ends on spur Road 100 off Road 3810.

THE TRAILS FROM SODA SPRINGS ROAD

Soda Springs Road parallels the south shore of Soda Springs Reservoir; turn off Highway 138 at Medicine Creek Road (Forest Road 4775, at the east end of the reservoir), and immediately turn left. Spur Road 012, the

Soda Springs Road, is a smooth-surfaced gravel road as far as Soda Springs Dam; beyond the dam, it is a rough track that can only be driven in a pickup truck or high ground-clearance automobile.

SODA SPRING TRAIL trailhead is a quarter of a mile from Highway 138; it passes under the powerhouse aqueduct and meanders out to the mineral spring that gives the reservoir its name.

BOULDER CREEK TRAIL starts at the gate blocking the end of Soda Springs Road. The trailhead has a vehicle turnaround and enough space for parking several automobiles.

The first part of the trail is a dirt-track road; a quarter of a mile down the trail is a fork; the left branch is Illahe Flat Trail, and the right branch is the continuation of Boulder Creek Trail. For the first mile or so past the fork, the trail is a steady switchbacked climb; it tops out on Pine Bench, a grassy plateau dotted with ponderosa pine. Early settlers on the North Umpqua cut hay on Pine Bench, hauled it out on horseback, and stored it to help feed their stock through the winter.

At the edge of Pine Bench, Bradley Trail branches off to the right. About a quarter of a mile farther on, a minor trail branches off to the left; follow the minor trail 100 yards to where a spring of water percolates out of the hillside; the water is cold enough to make your teeth hurt, and so sweet to the taste that drinking from the spring is enough of an excuse for climbing the hill.

Cautions: (1) Stay on the trail; the ground cover on rocky hillsides is fragile, and cutting across switchbacks hastens erosion. (2) Carry a canteen; the climb is steep, and you will want a drink of water long before you reach the top. (3) Both sides of the trail are carpeted with poison oak.

DOG CREEK INDIAN CAVES
(Bradley Ridge Trail No. 1551)

To reach the trailhead: Turn on Forest Road 4713 (about half a mile upstream from Island Campground on Highway 138); drive 4.2 miles and turn right on Road 100; drive 3 miles and turn right on Road 120; drive 3.6 miles and turn right on Road 130. The trailhead is marked with a sign, and is about one-half mile down Road 130 from the junction.

The roads to the trailhead are all well-surfaced, well-maintained gravel.

The upper end of Lough Mine Trail is on Road 120, three-tenths of a mile down from its junction with Road 100. The Lough's Mine is closer to the lower end of the trail; the trail is steep, and if you want to see Lough's mine, you should walk in from the bottom end of the trail. (If you walk in from the bottom, the trip out will all be downhill).

The Bradley Ridge Trail is a strenuous 1.6 mile hike through mixed Pacific madrone, oak, maple, and Douglas fir forest. The author and his wife first hiked the trail in late March; patches of snow dotted the hillside. The wildflowers were blooming; gray squirrels, deer, and birds were plentiful, and there were no mosquitoes or no-see-ums. In the first quarter mile, the trail gains about 80 feet in elevation; the next half mile is downhill and loses several hundred feet in elevation; the remainder of the trail is relatively flat. The steepest half mile of this trail is about a 30% slope — considerably steeper than the normal pitch of a house roof. The author walked in to the caves in about 25 minutes, but took an hour walking out uphill.

The caves are a hole in a volcanic lava dike and are actually a single large grotto about 50 feet wide and 20 feet high, extending back about 30 feet. The grotto is an eastern exposure, so it is protected from the prevailing summer and winter winds and bad weather. Three smaller recesses — probably dug out by hand, over the centuries, for bedrooms — open off the back of the grotto.

The first Forest Service exploring party, over half a century ago, reported that:

Refuse on the cave floor varied from a few inches to two or three feet in depth. This was composed mainly of dirt, deer hair, fragments of bones and numerous rocks which showed signs of having been subjected to intense heat. Chips of obsidian, which substance is not native to this district, were numerous. A few tiny arrowheads were found, but no systematic march for relics was made.... Shallow pits, where tepees once stood were found on a nearby ridge, indicating that the Dog Creek basin was once a popular hunting ground.

The walls are covered with pictures — most painted on with red pigment, and a few done in a bluish-colored pigment. The site has been excavated, and the artifacts have been removed, but you can see by the marks on the walls how high the dirt floor extended before excavation.

Walk out to the point of the lava dike (just beyond the caves) and on a clear day you'll be presented with a stunning view of the surrounding countryside.

Cautions: (1) The trail is probably too strenuous for small children and for anyone not in good health. Overweight people, if willing to set a leisurely pace, and if otherwise healthy, should have no problems. (2) Wear high-topped shoes that protect your ankles from twisting. (3) Carry insect repellant, a first aid kit, and a canteen of drinking water.

MEDICINE CREEK INDIAN CAVE

To reach the trailhead: Turn off Highway 138 at the upper end of Soda Springs Reservoir onto Medicine

Creek Road (Forest Road 4775). Drive 1.3 miles to the parking area on the right side of the road. Medicine Creek Road is paved and can be driven in a motorhome.

One-tenth of a mile before you reach the parking area, you will pass the Bradley Trail trailhead (F.S. Trail 1491) on the left. Bradley trail is one of the entries into the Boulder Creek Wilderness.

The Trail begins at a large boulder on the right, about 75 yards uphill from the parking lot, and is just a path up the hill to a large rock knob about 60 yards from the road.

The cave isn't really a cave, but just a pronounced overhang of rock that protects an area about 15 feet square from the elements. There are pictographs on the walls and roof, as at Dog Creek Caves.

Caution: Watch for poison oak.

Umpqua Hot Springs

There are several ways to reach Umpqua Hot Springs; the two easier ones are detailed here.

To reach the trailhead: Turn from Highway 138 onto Forest Road 34, the Toketee-Rigdon Road; follow the road past Toketee Reservoir until it forks; take the right fork (Forest Road 3401, the North Umpqua Road). The North Umpqua Trail (trial No. 1414) trailhead will be on your left as you approach the bridge over the North Umpqua River.

Or, continue on up Forest Road 3401 to approximately milepost 2. At milepost 2 there is a parking area, a footbridge across the North Umpqua River, and a trail that connects with Trail 1414 a few hundred yards downstream from the springs.

Both trails are new, well-cared for (so you can walk them in sneakers) and don't show up on most maps. The last few hundred yards of trail before you reach the springs is very steep, but the folks who constructed it thoughtfully built in several flat spots for rest stops.

The Hot Springs bubbles out of the side of the cliff that faces the north shore of the river. The Forest Service has constructed a gazebo over the springs, and has provided a pit toilet about 50 yards further up the trail.

Caution: On weekends, the hot springs are taken over by nudists; if the sight of nude strangers bothers you, you should restrict your visits to the middle of the day during the middle of the week.

Stan Knouse was a North Umpqua regular who loved the river and the fish and spent much time protecting both. Scott Ripley photo

SUSAN CREEK FALLS AND INDIAN MOUNDS

The trailhead is on Highway 138, directly across from the Susan Creek picnic area and raft launching site.

The trail is wide enough for two people to walk abreast, is well developed and maintained, and can be hiked in sneakers. The first three-quarters of a mile is an easy to moderate uphill climb; the next quarter of a mile is downhill to Susan Creek Falls, and the final quarter of a mile is a steep uphill climb to the Indian Mounds.

Susan Creek Falls pours over a rock face about 50 feet high. The falls isn't spectacular, but is pretty, and is an excellent place to picnic on a hot summer afternoon: because of the cool breeze from the falls, and the shade of the trees (the sun never shines on Susan Creek Falls), the canyon below the falls will be several degrees cooler than the surrounding area. A picnic site with a table and firepit overlooks the falls.

The Indian Mounds aren't really mounds at all, but piles of rocks. Among Native American cultures, a common rite of passage into manhood was a period of solitary fasting and vision-seeking. A boy would be sent off into the woods by himself to fast and seek places of power where he could counsel with and receive visions from spirits. The knob above Susan Creek Falls was one of the places of power commonly sought by the Indians who inhabited the North Umpqua region. The mounds are piles of rocks built up as a sort of meditative task by the boys who fasted and waited there for their visions.

Cautions: Stay on the trail! The trail from the falls to the Indian Mounds crosses a hillside carpeted with poison oak. Leave your dog in your car: it is impervious to the effects of poison oak, but its coat will pick up the irritant oil from the leaves, and pass it on to you when you pet the dog.

DOUGLAS COUNTY MUSEUM

The Douglas County Museum is located at the Douglas County Fairgrounds. Take the Fairgrounds exit (exit 123) from Interstate 5 and follow the signs.

The museum has Native American and natural history exhibits, exhibits illustrating Douglas County history, a research library, and a gift shop that sells everything from handmade crafts to books about Oregon and Douglas County. Douglas County museum is not dry and dusty, like some museums; its exhibits are lively, entertaining, and informative, and the staff are knowledgeable and helpful.

GLIDE WILDFLOWER SHOW

On the last full weekend in April each year, there is a wild plant show at the Glide Community Center.

Although called a wildflower show, its exhibits show much more than just a few nosegays of wildflowers. Some exhibits show a community of plants (such as the community of plants commonly seen in an alpine meadow or around a rock tarn) in its native habitat. All exhibits are marked with a descriptive card which tells the latin and common names of the plants and where they are found; and the cards are color-coded to show which plants are common, and which are rare or endangered.

Spend a day wandering through this show, looking at the exhibits and talking to the people who run them, and you can learn more than an armload of books can teach you.

Admission is free, but the sponsors will accept donations.

COLLIDING RIVERS

Very seldom will two rivers meet head on; the North Umpqua and Little River do at Glide. Colliding Rivers Park is at the intersection of Highway 138 and Glide Loop Road just east of milepost 17.

The park has a picnic site, a viewpoint for the colliding rivers, and nature information on markers throughout the park.

WINCHESTER DAM FISH LADDER

Take exit 129 from Interstate 5, park in the gravel parking lot at the north end of the Old Highway 99 bridge.

Oregon Department of Fish and Wildlife maintains a fish viewing station at the north end of the dam, where you can view anadromous fishes on their upstream spawning migration. Fall Chinook are likely to be passing over the ladder during October and November; spring Chinook during May and June; winter steelhead in January; summer steelhead from June to August; coho salmon in October; and sea-run cutthroat trout in October. You may also occasionally see resident river rainbow or cutthroat trout or non-game fishes, and, during the spring months, downstream migrant salmon or steelhead smolts on their way to the ocean.

ROCK CREEK FISH HATCHERY

Turn left off Highway 138 at the Rock Creek Hatchery sign just past milepost 22.

The lane into the hatchery parallels Rock Creek; watch the creek an hour or so when fish are moving up to the hatchery, and you can see how a salmon or steelhead moves through a hole of water, where it goes over a break, and what sort of cover it uses.

Rock Creek Hatchery supplies most of the hatchery fish stocked in the North Umpqua, and conducts much of the fisheries research done on Umpqua system fish runs. A visit to the hatchery gives you the chance to see everything from fingerlings to 30-pound Chinook close-up.

There are no signboards or audiovisuals at Rock Creek Hatchery to explain what you are seeing, but there are usually hatchery employees present who will answer your questions.

WATERFALLS

If you were so inclined, you could spend several days doing nothing but looking at waterfalls. There are several dozen in the North Umpqua drainage. The only thing the ones described below share in common is that they are easy to get to. Watson is the highest, and Toketee is the most terrifying. The others are food for the soul, there for the tasting.

Clearwater and Whitehorse

Clearwater and Whitehorse are both falls on the Clearwater River; both are adjacent to National Forest Campgrounds of the same names on Highway 138. While neither is particularly spectacular, both provide welcome refuges on hot summer afternoons: the babble of the falls drowns out the noise and bustle of the highway, the spray from the falls and the shade of the trees makes the air in the picnic areas several degrees cooler than the surrounding country, and the scenery makes the picnic areas a calming, restful place.

Toketee Falls

Toketee is the Chinook jargon word for pretty; it was first applied to the falls, and later to the reservoir near the falls.

To reach the trailhead — turn on the Toketee-Rigdon Road (Forest Road 34) at Toketee Junction. Drive about a quarter of a mile and turn left on the spur road at the Toketee Falls Trail sign. Spur road dead-ends at the trailhead.

A mammoth pipe, made of redwood staves held together by steel hoops, parallels the spur road to the trailhead. The pipe carries water 1663 feet from the Toketee Dam to an aqueduct through the mountainside; the flow rate in the pipe is approximately 9800 gallons per second. This pipe is a remnant of the original hydroelectric project, still in use after half a century.

There are picnic tables and pit toilets at the trailhead.

The trail is perhaps half a mile long, and, though steep enough to make the hike good exercise, is well enough surfaced and maintained that it can be hiked in sneakers. The trail parallels the river and for much of its length meanders through a forest of mixed hardwoods and evergreens. A few hundred yards of the trail hugs the edge of a precipice, and if you look down, you will appreciate the guardrail along the side of the trail. The viewpoint is a rail-enclosed platform cantilevered out from the hillside, and gives one the feeling of hanging suspended in midair.

The falls starts with a series of smaller falls, from a few feet to a few dozen feet in height; some can be seen from the trail. The main falls thunders over a precipice into a chasm hundreds of feet deep. The rock face that flanks the falls is columnar basalt — the remnant of a subsurface lava pool a which cooled slowly enough for hexagonal crystalline structures to form. The rock columns are the crystalline structure, and they assume their hexagonal shape because of their high quartz content.

Caution: Stay on the trail! If you get off the trail and lose your footing, you may fall anywhere from 50 to 200 feet before you hit bottom. Keep pets on a leash.

Watson Falls

To reach the trailhead: Turn south off Highway 138 onto Fish Creek Road (Forest Road 37); Watson Falls Picnic Grounds and Trailhead are a scant tenth of a mile from Highway 138. There is adequate parking for several vehicles, several picnic tables, and pit toilets at the trailhead.

The trail is wide and well-maintained, but climbs an estimated 300 vertical feet in three-tenths of a mile. There are two main viewpoints on the trail: the first is a rustic railed bridge across Watson Creek; the second, at the upper end of the trail, is a ledge on the side of the rock face the falls pours over. The falls — the upper end of Watson Creek Canyon terminates at a semicircular rock face about 300 feet high. Watson Creek roars off a notch in the top of the cliff to form the falls. According to the marker in the parking lot at the trailhead, Watson Falls is 272 feet high.

Cautions: Stay on the trail! There is no railing along the ledge that forms the upper viewpoint, so stay back from the edge. Keep pets on a leash.

Steamboat Creek Falls

Steamboat Creek actually has two falls the fish must overcome; the first is Little Falls, located adjacent to Steamboat Creek Road just upstream of milepost 1; the other is Steamboat Falls.

To reach Steamboat Falls, turn north off Highway 138 onto Steamboat Creek Road; turn right and cross the bridge at milepost 5; turn left on Road 3810 on the far side of the bridge and drive one mile to Steamboat Falls Camp.

The falls isn't much, as waterfalls go on the North Umpqua. Its big attraction is the steelhead and salmon that try to leap it: watch the falls on any warm afternoon between spring to autumn, and you will probably see anadromous fish trying to climb it. The government has built a bypassing fish ladder, but some fish still try to climb the falls.

ROADSIDE GEOLOGY

There's not much in the way of gemstones to be found along the North Umpqua, and since most of the drainage is closed to mineral location claims, mining for gold is illegal.

However, the rocks along the river do have an interesting history. Most of the rock formations are volcanic in origin. For instance, when you drive along Highway 138 or float down the river and pass high bluffs that look like grayish sand, you are looking at the result of the eructation that formed the caldera now known as Crater Lake. The Crater Lake rim and the island in Crater Lake are what remain of a large mountain (Mount Mazama) filled with the same sort of ash that spewed from Mt. St. Helens a few years ago: the mountain belched the loose ash out, leaving a hollow cone-shaped shell; lacking support for its weight, the crest of the cone collapsed on itself. The layer of ash is almost 100 feet thick in places along the upper end of the North Umpqua drainage, but that same layer of ash crops up a few inches thick in places as far east as Montana.

The floating rocks you find in the lakes along the North Umpqua are pumice — molten rock spit out of the volcano in chunks honeycombed with bubbles; the liquid rock solidified before the bubbles could surface and escape, and the trapped gasses in the bubbles make the rocks light enough to float.

The sharp spires of rock and the dikes — some of which look like rock fences when viewed from a distance — are examples of a type of rock that did not come from a surface eruption. The spires were likely formed when eruptions of the type that scattered the ash and pumice formed cone-shaped hills; such eruptions were sometimes followed by flows of superheated liquid rock of a denser type. The denser rock would push its way up through the hole or chimney in the center of the cone-shaped hill, and possibly coat the outside of the cone with a lava flow; when the lava stopped flowing, the liquid rock inside the chimney cooled slowly and became very hard and massive. Subsequent millions of years of wind, water, and natural cataclysms weathered away the softer rock of the cone and left standing the spire of harder rock that was once the chimney.

Dikes were formed similarly. The pressure of the molten rock trying to force its way to the surface caused a crack in the side of a volcanic cone; when the pressure lessened and the flow of lava through the crack stopped, the rock that solidified in the crack was harder than the rock that surrounded it and was left as a dike or rock wall after the cone weathered away.

There are a few outcrops of sedimentary rock along the North Umpqua, but such outcrops are more common farther west (in the valley), and especially in roadcuts along Interstate 5. These sediments are mostly shale — the gray mud and silt that lined the shallow seas that once covered most of the western United States.

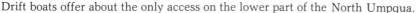

Drift boats offer about the only access on the lower part of the North Umpqua.

INDEX